Thomas Greenwood

A tour in the states & Canada. Out and home in six weeks

Thomas Greenwood

A tour in the states & Canada. Out and home in six weeks

ISBN/EAN: 9783337184759

Printed in Europe, USA, Canada, Australia, Japan

Cover: Foto ©Andreas Hilbeck / pixelio.de

More available books at **www.hansebooks.com**

A TOUR IN THE STATES & CANADA.

OUT AND HOME IN SIX WEEKS.

By Thomas Greenwood.

ILLUSTRATED.

London:
L. UPCOTT GILL, 170, STRAND, W.C.

PRINTED BY A. BRADLEY, 170, STRAND, LONDON.

PREFACE.

The New World is naturally a source of great interest to most English people, and there are few in the old country who have not friends or relatives in America. Much has been said and written of that country, but it covers such a vast area, its progress has been so rapid, and its future is so promising, that the subject is far from being yet exhausted. A "run over to the States" is a matter of far less importance, in these days of travel, than a journey from York to London was considered fifty years ago. In the way of many, however, who would like to see for themselves the state of things across the Atlantic, there are many obstacles, and to aid in the removing of a few of these, and to give some practical and useful information, has been the aim of

THE AUTHOR.

London,
    April, 1883.

CONTENTS.

	PAGE
PREFACE	iii

CHAPTER I.
| INTRODUCTION ... ... | 1 |

CHAPTER II.
| ACROSS THE ATLANTIC ... ... | 5 |

CHAPTER III.
| HOTELS AND HOTEL LIFE ... ... | 18 |

CHAPTER IV.
| AMERICAN RAILWAYS ... ... | 25 |

CHAPTER V.
| NEW YORK AND ITS SIGHTS ... ... | 30 |

CHAPTER VI.
| UP THE HUDSON ... ... | 39 |

CHAPTER VII.
| BOSTON ... ... | 43 |

CHAPTER VIII.

	PAGE
MONTREAL	51

CHAPTER IX.

SHOOTING THE RAPIDS	57

CHAPTER X.

QUEBEC AND OTTAWA	61

CHAPTER XI.

TORONTO	66

CHAPTER XII.

THE NIAGARA FALLS	69

CHAPTER XIII.

BUFFALO, CLEVELAND, AND DETROIT	74

CHAPTER XIV.

CHICAGO	79

CHAPTER XV.

CINCINNATI AND LOUISVILLE	85

CHAPTER XVI.

ST. LOUIS AND PITTSBURGH	89

CHAPTER XVII.

THE OIL REGIONS	94

CHAPTER XVIII.

RICHMOND AND BALTIMORE	101

Contents.

CHAPTER XIX.
Washington ... 105

CHAPTER XX.
Philadelphia ... 112

CHAPTER XXI.
Railroad Scenery of Pennsylvania ... 123

CHAPTER XXII.
Manufacturing Centres—Trenton ... 128

CHAPTER XXIII.
Manufacturing Centres—Paterson ... 138

CHAPTER XXIV.
Manufacturing Centres—Newark ... 142

CHAPTER XXV.
Manufacturing Centres—Providence and Hartford ... 145

CHAPTER XXVI.
General Impressions ... 150

CHAPTER XXVII.
Who should Emigrate ... 157

CHAPTER XXVIII.
Tariff Charges and Table of Distances, &c. ... 161

A TOUR IN
THE STATES AND CANADA.

CHAPTER I.

INTRODUCTION.

SEVERAL prominent excursion agents may reasonably claim to have created a vast amount of foreign travel. Thousands now make tours on the Continent who, a few years ago, were content to spend their annual holiday at some near watering place or other English pleasure resort. It is well that it should be so, for not only health and enlarged information accrue, but people of various nationalities are, by these means, becoming far better acquainted with each other than was the case twenty to forty years ago, and a great civilising power is thus at work which diplomatists of powder-and-shot proclivities will be compelled in the future to take into consideration. Popular, and deservedly so, as continental tours are, I have strong reasons for thinking that very many who thus spend their holiday do not know what might be done with a few weeks in a visit to the United States.

That such a tour would be gladly welcomed by thousands of business men. I am, from experience gained in moving about over the greater part of the three kingdoms, thoroughly convinced. The general feeling, however, with regard to it is that it would take so long to do, and that the journey would in itself be so costly, that these barriers stand in the way of its being undertaken. The object that I have now in view is to prove that neither obstacle need deter from a visit to the New World. The number of business and professional men who need rest and an absolute change is legion. To these let me seriously recommend crossing the Atlantic, and seeing for themselves the state of things generally in that immense country on the other side. Such a visit could not fail to be full of the greatest interest to the individual making it. Personally, I have accomplished on two occasions what I am now suggesting, and, of all the tours which I have made, those which have given me the greatest pleasure and general profit have been my six weeks' journeys to and from the States and Canada. My route and work were carefully planned beforehand, and, nothing occurring in any way to hinder my arrangements, I was enabled to be back again at business almost on the very day that I had calculated prior to sailing. To many, six weeks is not a long holiday, and for real enjoyment, coupled with all that can give rest and excite interest, commend me to a run over to America and back again.

My endeavour will be to give such practical hints and information that anyone following my suggestions may have a holiday which will never fade from memory ; and, if the time is properly used, the infusion of fresh ideas, in even such a hasty sight of our energetic cousins, can of itself scarcely fail to fully compensate for the pecuniary expense, which need not be by any means heavy.

Sea travelling has moved with the times, and for safety and comfort in locomotion I would sooner cross the Atlantic than go to Rome. The chief liners of this ocean service are as luxuriously furnished as many large hotels, and the conveniences are such as many who have never been on board an ocean steamer would little dream of. The carrying of the mails, and the rapidly-increasing number of Americans who now visit this country annually, enable the leading companies, by thus creating competition, to cater for every reasonable requirement. Coming over to Europe is a matter of such common occurrence in the States, that the education of our cousins—especially of commercial men—is looked upon as being scarcely completed until they have done so; and they undertake the tour as readily, and in hundreds of cases as regularly, as English people rush over to the Continent, and so aid to swell the great crowd that now yearly cross the Channel. Why there should not be as many from this side crossing the Atlantic as there are from the other side I fail to see, and, in course of years, as it becomes known how much may be done in a short time and far from extravagant outlay, I have not the slightest doubt but that this will be the case.

So much, again, is said of the competition of Americans and the rapid strides which they are making in their manufacturing industries, that, to see for oneself the actual state of things, and where they have advantages over us, should certainly be a good incentive to take an opportunity of forming opinions on these matters from personal observation.

Even if there is, to begin with, a dash of the "Oh! my!!" complaint—to use Mark Twain's expressive designation of sea sickness—it is really, in many cases at least, more beneficial to the system than otherwise. It enhances the enjoyment of the after part of the voyage, and gives a relish for meals that no amount of exercise on *terra firma* can do. Ten days' life on an ocean steamer is a holiday in itself. The freedom from post, telegraph, and newspapers is a luxury which only those who have experienced it can well appreciate. "Masterly inactivity" becomes the order of the day. The saloon library is a decided boon, and each passenger takes a vast interest in all the others. The amount of fraternising between the voyagers places far into the shade the most sociable "at home" or evening party which takes place on land. The exchange of opinions, developing into discussions more or less excitable on every imaginable topic, is a boon which to many a mind brings a decided change. The stereotyped grooves of daily life are quite departed from, and what would be considered trivial and commonplace, or even *infra dig.* at home, is at sea looked upon in quite a different light. The speed "she" is making, how the compass stands, sighting other vessels, the momentary views of whales or even a stray shark, the amusement growing out of watching shoals of porpoises with their comical Indian file habit of jumping out of the water, all afford a varied source of interest. Shuffleboard, nautical quoits, and probably a little dancing, constitute other amusements, played over and over again with a zest similar to that with which schoolboys enter into marbles and the numerous sports common to the playground.

The best months for crossing the Atlantic and for an agreeable tour on the other side are April, May, June, and the latter part of August, September, and October. The early or the later periods of these months should be selected if the intending voyager has a choice. The great heat of July and August, and sometimes of June, account for this, and a further reason is that the Americans are themselves taking their holidays during these months, so that anyone going there at these periods must expect to find churches closed, those to whom letters of introduction may be addressed gone out of town, theatres and kindred places of amusement undergoing repairs, and other drawbacks which need not now be discussed. From 95deg. to 100deg. Fahr. is a common heat in the sun during July and August, and I have, at that time of year, experienced 104deg. in the shade, but even this great heat I found far less oppressive and exhausting than ten to fifteen degrees less in England.

CHAPTER II.

ACROSS THE ATLANTIC.

THE choice of an ocean company, and particular ship, is necessarily most important. This account is not written with a view of making comparisons between the various lines of steamers; but as I desire to be practical in all I have to say, I may mention that my own choice has been the Cunard Company, and, however often I might be crossing, this line would be my selection. Much has been said and written recently about certain steamers having crossed from Queenstown to New York in a little over seven days, but speed is, after all, not the most admirable feature of sea travelling. Safety is, unquestionably, the matter of primary concern, and this is as near absolutely certain with the Cunard Company's steamers as is possible. For forty-two years they have had the proud boast of not having lost the life of a passenger, or even a letter; and, as I am writing more particularly for those who have never crossed the Atlantic, or, possibly, made any long sea voyage, I cannot do better than place before their notice the oldest and, in my humble estimation, the best of the ocean companies catering for this traffic. Again, what is an extra one or two days at sea in a journey of over three thousand miles? Steaming at high pressure speed may be, to some extent, amusing to captain and officers, but, as the facts of certain greatly lauded swift passages which have recently been made become widely known, the public will commit themselves very charily to such ships. I may incidentally mention that for one of these quick passages the consumption of coal was over 200 tons per day, that before leaving Liverpool she took on twenty extra stokers, and even these were insufficient for the work, the hands from the deck having to be sent down to their assistance. Further than this, she was dangerously near icebergs, as she was taking the most direct course, which would bring her into their neighbourhood, nearer than a more southerly course would have done. It appeared to me, in fact, just a question of drawing the line at a "color'd gent'man" sitting on the safety valve. The Cunard Company, while not claiming to have the fastest vessels afloat, have ships engaged in this trade which will more than compare with those of other competing companies. The average passage of their best boats from Liverpool to New York is from nine to ten days. The companies who advertise quick passages as their leading quality are careful to give the length of time taken in steaming from Queenstown to Sandy Hook, on the American side, or *vice versâ*, which means a difference of over twenty-four hours, as against the length of time from Liverpool to New York. Anyone intending to make such a tour as I purpose describing, and who selects one of the ships of the Cunard Company, cannot fail to observe why they have been so successful in avoiding accidents and loss of life. The minutest detail about the vessel and her navigation is most carefully attended to. Every man is appointed for his particular work, and that man specially selected for his experience and ability for that post. The officers are among the oldest in the Atlantic service, and, by liberal pay and good treatment, they endeavour not only to maintain their own reputation, but they have the interests of the Company thoroughly at heart,

The leading steamers of this company are the "Cephalonia," " Gallia," "Servia," "Bothnia," and "Scythia." The three first are very fine ships—in fact, simply floating palaces, containing every accommodation and requirement possible in sea travelling. The two last, by both of which I have crossed, are twin ships, and capital sea-going boats. With the view of diminishing the chances of collision, the steamers of this line take a specified course for all seasons of the year. On the outward passage from Queenstown to New York crossing meridian of 50 at 43 latitude, or nothing to the north of 43, and on the homeward passage crossing the meridian of 50 at 42 latitude, or nothing to the north of 42.

The rates are as follows: For saloon passengers, single tickets, 15, 18, 21, and 26 guineas, according to accommodation; return tickets, 30, 35, and 45 guineas. Saturday is the day on which the steamers leave Liverpool for New York, this being usually a very convenient day for commencing a holiday. The passage should be booked as early as possible before going, as the best state cabins are allotted in priority of application. It is advisable to secure a cabin as near the centre of the vessel as can be arranged. The difference in the fares I have named refers entirely to the position of the state cabin, *not* to the food supplied. This is exactly the same for all saloon passengers, and all use the same saloon. With the higher fares, two only would share the same state cabin, but with the lower fares there might, if passengers were numerous, be three, or even four.

The officers and stewards are most courteous and attentive, and personally I cherish some very agreeable acquaintances made among the officers of the Cunard Company, who are all picked men. On the boats I have named there is a captain and six officers, and even each of the under officers must have been first master of a ship before being eligible as fourth, fifth, or even sixth officer on board these leading liners.

The table is a most liberal one. There are three full meals, and supper is also supplied, but without the table being set out for it. In order to give something like a complete idea of how ample is the choice of dishes, the following bill of fare for a dinner when we were in mid-ocean on the "Scythia" will be interesting:

Soups.
Kidney and Tomato.
Fish.
Salmon and Lobster Sauce.

Entrées.
Haricot Ox Tail.   Fricassée Calf Head aux Tomatoes.
Giblet Pies.   Vegetable Stew.

Joints—Roast.
Beef and Baked Potatoes.
Haunch Mutton, Currant Jelly.   Hare, Brown Sauce.
Sucking Pig, Bread Sauce.
Turkeys, Cranberry Sauce.   Geese and Apple Sauce.

Joints—Boiled.
Corned Beef and Parsnips.
Fowls and Parsley Sauce.   Ox Tongue.

Vegetables.
Plain Boiled Potatoes.   Croquettes ditto.
Mashed Turnips.   Lima Beans.   Rice.

Entremets.
Bread and Butter Pudding.   Italian Creams.
Apple Charlotte.   Damson Vol-au-Vent.
Orange Mirlitons.

Dessert.
Apples, Pears, Pineapple, Oranges.
Barcelona Nuts.   Almonds and Raisins.
Tea and Coffee.

The choice for breakfast (8.30 a.m. to 10 a.m.) and lunch (1 o'clock) is just as complete as can be wished for such meals.

The same seat at table is retained during the whole voyage, and so the gathering soon becomes of quite a family character, the same faces being seen at every meal, unless, from motives of domestic economy, the said faces be conspicuous by their absence. These opportunities of forming acquaintances are really to be appreciated. It is very probable that at the seasons of the year to which I have referred there will be among the passengers some representing almost every European nationality, and again likely that there will be some of these who have travelled over the greater portion of the whole world. On a recent voyage, we had Swedes, Frenchmen, Belgians, Germans, and Spaniards, as well as Canadians and Americans, thus illustrating the great popularity of the company I have named.

It is wonderful how communicative people become at sea. Being thrown on each other's and on their individual resources for a period of some ten days aids considerably in cultivating a general desire to be agreeable, and to give and receive information. In connection with this matter, I may state that on my return voyage in May we had a celebrated English Arctic explorer, who gave us in the saloon, on one of the evenings at sea, a most interesting lecture on Arctic travelling, a collection being made afterwards in aid of the Orphanage for Seamen's Children. There is invariably either an impromptu entertainment or concert got up on every voyage for the benefit of this admirable institution, and the ladies, as a rule, take up the gifts, as, for some peculiar reason, it is known that the pockets of the gentlemen present suffer far more severely when a lady carries the plate, than when those of the male persuasion take this duty in hand. Anyone given to making friends and acquaintances cannot fail to greatly enjoy the opportunities afforded in this direction.

As I have already said, a sea voyage is in every sense a real holiday—to those, of course, who have no great dread of sea-sickness, and who stand a good chance of picking up their sea legs, say, by the beginning of the third day out. To a business man, who has had a year of commercial worry, and who feels that his physical machinery requires bracing up, I do not know of any better way by which such a happy result can be arrived at than by the absolute change that accrues from a sea voyage. If I may digress for a moment, it is only to say that after my return from the States I felt so benefited in health that I strongly urged two commercial friends (each of whom had, during two or three winters, attacks of blood-spitting and a tendency to chest weakness and general debility, which might eventually have proved serious) to take such a trip as I had made, and although this is now several years ago, after adopting the plan they attributed entirely to this voyage a thoroughly recruited state of health.

The question of sea-sickness is, of course, a vital one to many. Unless there is some natural constitutional weakness which makes the complaint habitual when travelling by water, there is really nothing in itself to deter anyone from making the voyage. Many cures and preventatives have been suggested. All may prove fruitless if the stomach is out of order, and, in that case, the sooner there is a clearance the better. Pyretic Saline is an almost indispensable article for a sea voyage. In many instances it will prevent sickness, and in other cases greatly alleviate it. If not accustomed to sea travelling, it is well to avoid a great mixture of foods. The choice at meals is so ample that a little dieting is very necessary until the traveller is safe on his sea legs. The cabin steward will bring anything needed to the berth. The more abstemiousness with regard to intoxicants is exercised, the better. Spirits, especially, certainly do not prevent or reduce sickness, except in rare individual instances. Hard biscuits and water are an old sea captain's remedy, until the system has become accustomed to the motion of the vessel. Lying flat on the back allays sickness wonderfully. A tight bandage of silk, or other material, fastened round the waist is another capital precaution. A pillow or bag, usually termed at sea a "bedfellow," to wedge yourself in your berth if the ship is rolling much, is also a thing worth remembering. It is advisable to secure the upper berth, if possible, for if your companion should be sick, it is obviously preferable to be above than below him.

There is generally a great deal of card-playing during the voyage, whichever line is selected, and there are invariably some good players at the peculiarly American game of "poker." There is no denying that money is played for in large sums, although beans may be the ostensible things which change hands.

There are few voyages in which a considerable sum is not lost and won, and my advice is to have nothing to do with such games. Betting on the speed "she" is making daily is another Atlantic "sin;" a pool is every day got up by some enterprising individual or other for those who feel so inclined. According to the tastes of the tourist he will invest, or not invest, irrespective of anything which I might suggest.

In addition to the other matters to which I have referred as aiding to pass the time pleasantly during the voyage, further plans will suggest themselves very readily to anyone who goes out with a view of securing the fullest enjoyment from the passage. The smoke-room, the chief rendezvous, of course, of the gentlemen, is usually the scene of much impromptu fun and smart repartee, and woe be to the individual who in this sanctum has got the name of "stringing the long bow," or "flinging the hatchet" in a conversational sense, for he is sure, for his exaggerations and uncertain facts and information, to be drawn out and exposed.

In moving up and down "the companion" and along the corridors, it is well for a novice in sea travelling not to be too venturesome. Keep a fast hold of the hand-rail, especially of the one to the staircase leading from the saloon up to the deck, known in nautical phraseology as above stated. I have in mind one gentleman who, on account of ignoring this little precaution, had a rib broken.

In the saloons and state cabins of the leading vessels of the Cunard Company there are electric bells, so that there is quick communication with the stewards. At the end of the voyage it is customary to give the table steward and the cabin steward, who have attended on your wants, a small fee—ten shillings each is a usual sum, less or more as the tourist may be disposed; it is not compulsory, but in most cases it is cheerfully paid on account of attentive and obliging service.

A word of advice here as to "keeping time" at sea. In

journeying westward—that is, from Liverpool to New York—the time is slower, so that a steamer of ordinary speed loses about half an hour each day of the running time with which she is charged, and in the journey home (eastward) gains a corresponding period. Attempting to keep the watch with the ship's time would thus necessitate putting backward or forward the timepiece, and so, perhaps, seriously injuring it. The better plan is to let the works run down, and depend upon the ship's bell and the saloon clock for the time. The "bell time" at sea will soon be mastered, and the passengers become accustomed to speaking of "four," "six," and "eight bells," as the case may be, as they would on land say "two," "three," and "four" o'clock, or the other hours which a given number of strokes represent. In order to be more explicit, the following statement will be of service. Commencing the day at sea with the half hour after midnight, the strokes of the bell will be:

1 bell .... $\frac{1}{2}$ o'clock a.m.	5 bells .... $6\frac{1}{2}$ o'clock a.m.
2 bells .... 1 ,, ,,	6 ,, ... 7 ,, ,,
3 ,, ... $1\frac{1}{2}$,, ,,	7 ,, ... $7\frac{1}{2}$,, ,,
4 ,, ... 2 ,, ,,	8 ,, ... 8 ,, ,,
5 ,, ... $2\frac{1}{2}$,, ,,	1 bell .... $8\frac{1}{2}$,, ,,
6 ,, ... 3 ,, ,,	2 bells .... 9 ,, ,,
7 ,, ... $3\frac{1}{2}$,, ,,	3 ,, ... $9\frac{1}{2}$,, ,,
8 ,, ... 4 ,, ,,	4 ,, ... 10 ,, ,,
1 bell .... $4\frac{1}{2}$,, ,,	5 ,, ... $10\frac{1}{2}$,, ,,
2 bells .... 5 ,, ,,	6 ,, ... 11 ,, ,,
3 ,, ... $5\frac{1}{2}$,, ,,	7 ,, ... $11\frac{1}{2}$,, ,,
4 ,, ... 6 ,, ,,	8 ,, ... 12 noon.

Then repeat in the same order for the second twelve hours.

The ship's library is, as a rule, a carefully selected one. Old voyagers make a speedy visit to the book-shelves after leaving port, and select according to taste. This plan affords a better choice than when some score of others have thinned the shelves by taking to their state rooms whatever they wish to read. A hint to the wise will be sufficient. It is scarcely necessary for me to advise the intending voyager not to spend too much time reading in the saloon if the weather is at all good. To pass as much time on deck as possible will be the aim of most, as this is not only conducive to making the voyage enjoyable, but certainly aids very considerably in keeping off or alleviating what to many is looked upon as a dreadful malady—the *mal de mer.*

Baggage.

Luggage is an important consideration in any tour, but it is doubly so in a brief trip to the States and back. It is advisable to mimimise it to the fullest extent if a short stay only is intended. A warm overcoat and a travelling rug should be taken for use during the voyage, as the air is often very keen, especially in the early mornings and in the evenings. A good sized Gladstone bag or portmanteau should afford enough room for the ordinary paraphernalia which a tourist desires to take with him, but if a longer stay is intended, a trunk or additional portmanteau will be necessary. The idea has long been exploded of the proverbial traveller coming over with luggage represented by a toothpick and a paper collar, for the personal belongings of a large number who visit Europe can in many cases scarcely be contained in two or three monster Saratoga trunks, and as many portmanteaus. A tourist suit, for travelling and lounging about the deck in, is indispensable, and woollen underclothing for wear during the voyage, for the reason stated above, will also be found useful. By all means reduce the quantity as low as possible, for moving luggage about in the States is an expensive item, unless carefully watched. Cab fares are exorbitantly dear; as much as six shillings being an ordinary fare for less than a mile, and I have known three dollars, or twelve shillings, charged for a fraction over a mile. What other means of locomotion and dealing with luggage there are I will refer to later, but I mention this matter of cabs now to show how politic it is to keep the quantity of baggage within narrow limits. A further reason is that the Customs'-house officers are sometimes capricious, and not disposed to view too liberally "personal effects," especially jewellery and a superabundance of other small property. At the same time, it should be borne in mind that the getting up of linen is very dear, and that every article of neck-wear, underclothing, clothes, hats, hosiery, boots, &c., is about double the price the same article would be with us, so that a sufficient supply should be taken to avoid having to purchase or being at the mercy of the washerwoman.

A good opera glass would be found useful, not only during the voyage, but on the other side when travelling by rail or water.

Money.

It is not necessary to get any American money before leaving England. Take for use on the other side English gold or Bank of England notes. The purser of the ship will change a few pounds for first requirements. The rate of exchange varies from 4·75 dols. to 4·85 dols. to the pound sterling. The tourist will very soon become accustomed to dollars and cents., the decimal system being simple and easily mastered. The Cunard Company give notes of exchange up to £20 free to passengers by their steamers, payable on presentation to their New York agents. Letters of credit, where a long tour is contemplated, will be found useful, and care should be taken to have these drawn on the best banks. The hotel proprietors will readily exchange American money for English gold or notes, or take same in payment of bills. With regard to the total cash requirements for the tour, all depends on the tourist himself. I have known £20 be sufficient for three weeks' travelling and hotel expenses when in the States. Thirty to forty pounds would amply serve, unless surplus items were allowed to accumulate, and for each extra week over this period say £7 to £10, according to the distances which are covered. I purpose, however, to give some tables of expenses which will enable an intending tourist to gauge within a little what charges he is likely to meet. It will be advisable that a little more money be taken than may be actually required. To find oneself with an insufficient supply of the "needful" when moving about in one's own country is embarrassing enough, but in a foreign land would be far from pleasant.

Landing.

About the ninth day out the event of the day will be the taking on of the pilot, who generally brings with him a supply of newspapers of various dates. Immediately these are in the smoke room they are seized, and the leading news of what has occurred during the time spent at sea is retailed out as it is noticed by those who have secured copies of the papers. During the last few days of the voyage there will be placed on the saloon tables railway maps, hotel cards, and other miscellaneous literature of a like character. It is well to pack up in good time, but in doing so it should be remembered that your luggage will have to be examined by the Customs'-house officers on landing, so that keys of trunks, bags, &c., should be kept as handy as possible. Your first sight of the New World will be Long Island and Fire Island, and very soon afterwards you will be in the Hudson River, and the medical officer and the Customs' officials will board your steamer. With the former you will have, personally, nothing to do; but the steerage passengers will have to pass by him in single file, and exhibit, as a species of passport, their certificates of vaccination, without which they would not be allowed to land. The doctor of your ship—and every vessel carries a duly certified surgeon—is, of course, present during this inspection. After that is over, the officers of the Revenue Department will seat themselves in the saloon, and passengers will file past. The questions are :

Name ?
Number of Packages ?
What description of Packages ?

If you have anything liable to duty, you will have to declare it, and all outside "personal effects" are liable to duties, which vary from 20 per cent. to 60 per cent. on the value. At the end of the book will be found a table showing some of the Customs' rates. The marvel is that the great American people, who claim to be the most enlightened nation in the world, should so meekly stand these enormous duties. Everything is taxed, and if you wish to see what it means, study the prices in the shop windows, or, if you do not see sufficient to convince you there, make inquiries, and you will learn enough to make you thankful that you belong to a Free Trade country, or I greatly mistake.

The gigantic sum of £30,000,000 is raised annually from the customs duties *over and above* what is required for the expenses of government. As to what becomes of this vast sum I would advise you to make inquiries when in America. The answer that I have always had to the question has been, "The professional politicians know best—ask them."

Every passenger has to see after his own luggage. The stewards will carry it on deck, and even on the landing stage, but you will have to take the small packages to the officer who has possession of the form bearing the number corresponding with that of the ticket which had been given to you on the ship. After this not always tender-hearted official has very gently (?) turned topsy-turvy the contents of your packages, he will very generously leave you to pack up again on a floor not always noted for its cleanliness.

Before leaving the ship decide as to which hotel you will go. "Garrett's" Express representative will be in attendance, and, after your luggage has been examined, call for him, and he will take all of it to the hotel selected, and you will find it there on your arrival. He will give you a receipt for the number of packages, and you will pay in your hotel bill for this conveying of your chattels at the following rates: Half a dollar (2s.) for each trunk or portmanteau, and the same sum for two bags, or bag and bundle of rugs.

The system of "expressing baggage" is a most convenient one in the States. By adopting this plan on landing, it leaves you quite free to walk to the hotel, or to follow any other course which may be agreeable. Do not be alarmed if the luggage does not reach the hotel before you, providing that you go direct there. "Garrett's" man is perfectly safe, and you can fully depend on its reaching its destination.

CHAPTER III.

HOTELS AND HOTEL LIFE.

AMERICAN hotels differ in many respects from those on this side the Atlantic. Our cousins over the "herring-pond" have strong leanings towards hotel life, and if the statistics could only be arrived at of the number who board and live entirely in them, it would convey to many in England a singular state of things. The usual method adopted, when a couple decide to get married, is, instead of furnishing and setting up as housekeepers, to go to board at some hotel, where all the cares and worries of domestic life are perhaps avoided, and where everything works according to system, with no servants to scold, and the wife's hands are not soiled (?) in pastry-making and other domestic operations. Ladies come down to breakfast in silks and satins, and children are neat and prim, fresh from the nurses' hands. From this universal patronage of hotels, they have been enabled to establish the "biggest things" in this line of any country in the world. Not a few commercial men, again, will have a bed and sitting room in some of the more fashionable parts of the city, and get all their meals in a convenient hotel. Whole families board and live in hotels, in some cases having private sitting-rooms, in other cases sharing the general parlours, which are usually most luxuriously furnished. These are, to all intents and purposes, their home, and in not a few instances the only home that many children know.

The Americans argue that the friction of domestic life is thus obviated—that it saves trouble, enables them to estimate exactly their expenses, and is altogether in accordance with their go-a-head proclivities. This may be so, but it destroys the very structure of domestic life. There is, in fact, little home life in the large cities of the States; and I am compelled to believe that the system is a pernicious one, breeding, as it unquestionably does, boldness and masculinity, if I may use the word, in the ladies, and unattractive precocity in the children.

That the hotels are well managed is very certain; that the table is good, and the food well cooked and served, all who have been in them will readily admit. There are many hotels, and the number is a growing one, which are conducted on the European plan—this means paying a certain price for room and each meal—but hotels conducted on the customary system of the country, the American plan, signify a fixed price for bedroom and three consecutive meals per day. This enables all visiting them to calculate exactly what they will have to pay, so that there need be no uneasiness as to whether "extras"—a very comprehensive phrase so far as many hotels are concerned on this side—will help to swell the bill. For three meals and a room the prices all over the States are 3dols., 3dols. 50c., or 4dols. per day. The higher rate (sixteen shillings per day) is for a bedroom on the second or third floor; 3dols. 50c. (fourteen shillings) per day for a room on the fourth floor; and 3dols. (twelve shillings) for bedroom on one of the other floors. As there is an elevator in nearly all the hotels, always in use, the height of the floors is not really felt. The meals are the same in all cases. When entering the hotel the name is registered, and it is most advisable to understand distinctly what is the rate at which you will have to pay.

Many of the hotels are so large that an accommodation of five hundred to a thousand bedrooms is not exceptional. The office, reading and smoking rooms, are on the ground floor, where the lavatory, shaving, and hair-cutting departments, telegraph and railway ticket offices are usually situated. On the first floor, as a rule, are the dining and breakfast rooms, and ladies' and gentlemen's parlours.

No one can complain on the score of the choice of dishes at American hotels. It is so ample that it is almost bewildering, and the most epicurean taste could not fail to be satisfied. In order to show that such is the case, and as a matter of general interest, the following copies of menus (not of a picked day or specially-selected house) will give a good general idea. It will be unnecessary, too, for me to give more than two out of the four meals per diem—breakfast and dinner—as being indicative of what lunch, served at 12.30 to 2.30, and supper, 7 to 11.30 p.m., are like. These two meals are just as elaborate as the others for choice. Raw oysters form one dish of almost everyone who sits down at lunch, and of this very palatable and nutritious shell-fish there is the most abundant supply—fried, stewed, and pickled, or raw, as may be desired.

BREAKFAST, 6 TO 11 A.M.

Oranges.

Broiled.

Beefsteak. Kidneys. Ham. Breakfast Bacon.
Mutton Chops. Jersey Pork Chops.
Calf's Liver. Pig's Feet. Country Sausages. Tripe.

Fish.

Codfish Balls. Shad. Live Codfish Steaks.
Panfish. Codfish with cream. Passaic Smelts.
Smoked Salmon. Fried Eels. Salt Mackerel.
Fried Saddle Rock Oysters.

Fried.

Ham and Eggs. Hominy. Liver and Bacon.
Tripe. Pigs' Feet.
Corned Beef Hash, browned. Frizzled Beef with Eggs.

Stewed.

Chicken. Oysters. Kidneys. Tripe.

Eggs.

Boiled.   Fried.   Scrambled.   Poached.
Omelette, plain, with ham, onions, parsley, jelly, and a l'Espagnole.

Cold.

Beef.   Mutton.   Ham.   Tongue.   Corned Beef.

Potatoes.

Boiled.   Baked.   Fried.   Sautée.   Saratoga Chips.
Hashed with cream.   Lyonnaise.

Bread, &c.

Hot Corn Bread.   Boston Brown Bread.   Vienna Rolls.
Hot Rolls.   Milk and Buttered Toast.
Graham Rolls.   Griddle Cakes.   Wheaten Grits.
Hominy.   Irish Oatmeal.   Boiled Rice.

Coffee.   English Breakfast Tea.   Green Tea.
Oolong Tea.   Chocolate.

DINNER, 5 TO 7 P.M.

Soups.

Chicken with rice.   Consommé Distillac.

Fish.

Kennebec Salmon baked with cream.   Potatoes à la Brabant.

Relèves.

Breast of Veal farcie à l'Anglaise.
Baked Pork and Beans, Boston style.

Entrées.

Fillet of Beef piqué a l'Impériale.
Sweetbread Croquettes with French peas.
Timbale of Chicken aux champignons.
Calf's Brains breaded, tartar sauce.

Roast.

Ribs of Prime Beef.   Spring Lamb, mint sauce.
Chicken with watercress.   Ham, champagne sauce.

Cold Dishes.

Pâté de Strasbourg.   Ham.   Pâté de Foie-gras.
Roast Mutton.   Tongue.   Roast Beef.

Bermuda Beets.   Potato Salad.   Spanish Olives.
Watercress.

<table>
<tr><td>Lobster.</td><td>Mayonnaise.
Jersey Lettuce.</td><td>Chicken.</td></tr>
</table>

Vegetables.

<table>
<tr><td>Onions, cream sauce.
Boiled Potatoes.</td><td>Green Peas.
Fried Parsnips.
Spinach au jus.</td><td>Stewed Tomatoes.
Mashed Potatoes.
Boiled Rice.</td></tr>
</table>

Pastry and Dessert.

Plum Pudding, brandy and hard sauce.
Sliced Apple Pie.   Greengage Tartelettes.
Mixed Candies.   Charlotte Russe à la Chantilly.
Petits Fours.   Macaroons Marseillaise.   Neapolitan Ice Cream.
Fruits in Season.   Nuts and Raisins.
English Cheese.   Roquefort Cheese.
French Coffee.

The coloured waiters are, as a rule, most attentive, and, although some feeing is done, it is not at all general, and a good and quick attention to orders may be relied upon.

I can now indicate a few hotels only where such accommodation as that I have been describing may be secured, and in naming them I wish it to be distinctly understood that neither the publisher nor myself have the least interest in doing so. There are others in addition to those I purpose naming which are equally good, but as it is an advantage to know and be able to decide upon a particular hotel beforehand, the following are now given with this practical object in view:

New York Hotels.—" The Grand Central," 667 to 677, Broadway; "Grand Union," opposite Grand Central Depôt; "International," opposite General Post Office; "Metropolitan," Broadway; "St. James's," Union-square. Any of these may be selected with confidence. They are all conveniently situated in the "Up Town" direction—that is, the more fashionable and residential part of New York. "Down Town" is the business portion of the city.

There are, of course, many other hotels which could be named, and I have no object in mentioning those above and not others, but from them there is sufficient choice. It is possible to obtain good accommodation at 10s. per day for room and meals, but the table in these cases would necessarily be less elaborate than the specimen *menu* cards which I have quoted. So far as New York is concerned, in addition to the leading hotels which could be named, there are upwards of 150 others of all grades, and at these board and lodging can be obtained at from 28s. to £3 per week.

I have thought it requisite to give an idea of only two meals, such as the bill of fare contained on one of the days I was staying at a New York hotel. Its comprehensive choice is indicative of what might be expected at most hotels charging the tariff referred to in the leading cities. Some towns, however, are lamentably lacking in good hotel accommodation, and in proof of this I might instance Pittsburgh. All the leading hotels of different cities are very much the same in character and management. There is always plenty of life and activity about them. Some are notoriously "political" houses, frequented by members of Congress and the scores of wire-pullers who are always to be found in their immediate neighbourhood.

I may say that the bill commences from the meal on the table at the time of entering the hotel, and that the rates I have named are for three *consecutive* meals per day—that is, breakfast, lunch, and dinner, or breakfast, early dinner, and supper. Four meals are actually laid, but if the whole are partaken of there will be an extra one charged. No allowance is made if you do not sit down to any of them. In some respects it may be inconvenient to be away sight-seeing, and have to come to the meals; but even with those hotels conducted on the European plan the charges for the meals are such that it just amounts to about the same as the fixed sum per day for those on the American plan.

Of American hotel life itself opinions would differ. In the parlours, furnished, as I have said, in a most superb manner, it is an exceptional thing to find a book; but this is easily accounted for by the fact of the company in them being very general, so that book literature for the use of guests would be too much to expect. There are, of course, files of newspapers in the reading or writing rooms of all hotels. To the credit of American hotels let it be said that there is little apparent drinking in them. It is the exception, and not the rule, to see wine taken at meals, and it would, I feel sure, be also readily granted by all who have visited the States, that there is far less open intemperance than is to be seen in some of our principal towns.

A word of advice here will not be out of place—avoid partaking too liberally of iced water. The very first thing set before a guest in every hotel and restaurant is a glass of iced water, and in the hot months this is very acceptable. Filters containing it are also scattered about the hotel, and if you are at all disposed you may have iced tea, iced milk in abundance, and a variety of other drinks, treated in a similar way, too numerous to mention. If you indulge too freely you may have visions and dreams of a dentist, so beware! You will soon discover that the dental profession is one of the most profitable in the States, and it is the excessive use of iced drinks, followed often by hot rolls, hot bread, and other foods, which makes this simply inevitable.

CHAPTER IV.

AMERICAN RAILWAYS.

OF the relative merits of English and American railways, and whether travelling is more comfortable in the States than with us and on the Continent, there is a wide diversity of opinion. In some respects the Americans have the advantage, but in other important details we certainly can claim it. First, and perhaps most important, is the matter of the depôts, or stations, as we are accustomed to designate them. At those in America there is no pretence of a platform, and as the officials are often not very numerous, it is no difficult matter for a stranger to take his seat in the wrong train, concerning which, when it is ready to start, there is no proper signalling off, but the conductor simply calls out, "All aboard?" and in a second the train is off. Those visiting the States must look out for this "All aboard?" and be careful that they do not lose a moment in getting on the platform of the train.

The great principle upon which life exists in America is that the public must look after themselves, and if they do not or cannot, the State will not do so for them. This specially applies to railways. There are no bridges over crossings, unless in rare instances, but simply a board bearing the injunction, "Railroad Crossing.—Beware of the Engine." The railways cross and run along some of the principal streets, and in Philadelphia and some parts of Boston, and many other cities, a miscellaneous crowd of foot passengers and vehicles waits on each side the rails until the train has passed.

The Grand Central Depôt in New York City is perhaps the finest and largest depôt in the States. Money was lavished on it, and yet for conveniences it is far behind the termini of most of the railways running into London. The restaurant at this large station is nothing more than a cellar, and the same may be said of some other depôts in New York, where a meal not only costs about five times as much as it should, but is miserably served. I was struck with this at the New Jersey central depôt, where passengers leave for Chicago and the Western cities. The buffet is a counter, dirty and diminutive, and the food—supplied, when I was there, by one coloured man and a boy—was such that, on any other visit that I may make, unless I happen to be starving, it will not have me for a customer again. When these depôts are contrasted with St. Pancras or King's Cross, or New-street, Birmingham; London-road Station, Manchester; or Lime-street, Liverpool. for conveniences and accommodation, they come out the worse for the comparison. There are no obliging railway porters who will, for a few coppers, take your small belongings and find out for you a comfortable corner. The passengers on the American railways walk down the long passage of the Pullman cars, loaded with their small packages, and stow them away as best they may.

The Pullman day drawing-room and the sleeping cars are luxuriously furnished and in every way convenient. These are charged extra to the ordinary fares, according to the distance travelled. From 2dols. to 4dols. additional may be accepted as a criterion. The Pullman is really the American first class, and that next it, designated on all the American railways as first, is the only one which those visitors at all likely to go out simply on a tour would care to make use of. These are the long cars with a passage down the centre, and reversible cushioned seats on either side to hold two in each. In every carriage are a lavatory and stove, and the latter, even in April, is often kept burning with anthracite coal to a most unbearable heat. When once in the train there is little chance of going wrong, as the conductor walks from end to end of it between each station. There is always company in the carriage, and no chance of molestation in any way, night or day, unless, of course, a man courts it. The company is necessarily of a mixed character, but that is of no consequence in travelling by American lines. There may be a baby or two, but there will be no drinking from flasks, no rowdyism, and I am bound to say I never yet saw an American placing his feet on the cushion of the opposite seat in close proximity to a lady's dress, as has often been described as a peculiarly American mode of expressing manly independence.

At certain stations the conductor will call out, "Fifteen (or twenty) minutes for breakfast," dinner, or supper, as the case may be, and at all the depots where the trains are fixed to stop in this way there is a marked difference in the accommodation provided and the food supplied, from what I have mentioned as being the case at the two New York depots specially named. The usual charge for sitting down to breakfast or supper at these restaurants is from half-a-dollar to a dollar, and for dinner from one to two dollars, and the food is, as a rule, both good and well served.

There is a peripatetic bookseller on every train who brings round newspapers, books, and magazines, and, by way of change, fruit and candy; he walks from one end of the train to the other, pushing his wares with the enterprise peculiar to the country, and in a way that will sometimes strike the stranger as being very odd.

The baggage system in operation on the American railways is decidedly the best for long journeys, but for the many short journeys on our English railways it is scarcely applicable. It is only necessary for the passenger to have his luggage taken to the baggage office, and there he can have it checked to whatever station he likes; he holds as a receipt for his packages brass checks, bearing numbers which correspond with the numbered checks on his luggage. The passenger need not take the slightest trouble about his luggage during the journey, for on reaching the end of it he has only to present these brass checks, or hand them to an " Express " agent (who enters the train several stations before arriving at a large town), and this official will take the luggage to wherever one wishes. Should the traveller desire to break his journey—as there is every facility for doing, intimation only requiring to be given to the conductor, who will endorse the ticket—the luggage will be kept at the station to where it has been checked, and it is impossible for anyone else to obtain it without the brass tokens in possession of the owner. This is an admirable system, and works remarkably well in the States, saving, as it does, all the worry of seeing baggage labelled and looking after it when there are changes at junctions.

The speed of the trains on the American railways is not so great as with us, and there are few trains for the long journeys, but this is not to be wondered at, considering the immense mileage of many of the companies. The trestle bridges over rivers and ravines will greatly interest the traveller who is in America for the first time, unless he happens to be of a very nervous temperament; but all persons, whether nervous or not, I would advise not to remain outside on the platform of the carriage when the train is running.

In order to accomplish as much as possible in a limited time, it will be necessary to do a little night travelling, but this to many would not be a hardship. The Pullman sleeping cars are quite as comfortable as a bed at an hotel. If the traveller is not disposed to go to the expense of two dollars per night extra for these, he will be able to make himself comfortable in the first-class carriage with a rug and an air pillow. He will have the consolation of not finding himself alone any time during the journey.

With regard to fares, I have given at the end of the book a table of rates to the leading places, but for first class the average in the Middle States and New England is 1d. to 1¼d. per mile, and from 1½d. to 2½d. per mile in the Western and Southern States, with the extra sum, as already named, for the Pullman sleeping or day drawing-room cars. Where there is strong competition the fares are lower. During the early months of 1882, so great was the competition between two companies, that each carried passengers from New York to Chicago for 3dols., or 12s. The usual sum was, however, charged for the return journey by both companies.

Tickets can be purchased at most hotels or ticket establishments, or even from the conductor on the train. Do not buy from the ticket "smashers" or "jobbers" who hang about some railway depots.

It will be useful to know that an "air route," which the tourist will see well advertised all over the States, means a direct line; and a "lightning express" is simply a fast train.

CHAPTER V.

NEW YORK AND ITS SIGHTS.

I HAVE already referred to the matter of cab fares. These are exorbitantly dear, and in all cases when hiring them it is most necessary to make the bargain beforehand; but even by so doing the price will seem not only excessive but most unjustifiable. Six shillings (1dol. 50cents) is quite an ordinary fare for a short distance, and I have known 3 dols., or 12s., paid for a fraction over a mile, so that those hiring them will require to know what they are about, or a few pounds in Jehus will very soon melt. There is, however, a splendid service of tramcars—"horse cars" they are termed in the States—stages, or omnibuses, and the overhead railroad, of which an engraving is given on page 31. This latter is a novelty which no other city in the world presents. The line now almost encircles the city, and the rails are on a level with the second-floor windows of the houses and places of business, and in some streets higher than this. Although accidents are not at all common on the line, personally I prefer the tramcars, which in many streets run underneath the ironwork of the "L" road, as the railway is called. The speed, of course, is not so great as by rail. The fare is 10 cents (5d.) for any distance by the railway, and by the tramcars 5 cents, or $2\frac{1}{2}$d. The streets in New York and other leading cities, as all know who have read of America, intersect each other at right angles, and there is a perfect network of tramways along these, so that there is no difficulty in reaching any part of the city. Broadway and Fifth-avenue are the principal streets where the tramway is not laid, and along these thoroughfares there are running the stages, drawn by two horses, to which I have referred. These have no conductor, the man on the box acting in the double capacity of driver and conductor. Passengers drop their fare (5 cents for any distance) into a box placed so that the

OVERHEAD RAILWAY, NEW YORK.

driver can see it. If change is wanted, it can be obtained from the driver, who passes it in sealed envelopes in convenient sums through a little hole, and the person requiring this opens the envelope and drops the right fare in the box. A more effectual way of preventing peculation it would be impossible to imagine. Passengers thus look after themselves, hailing the stage or stopping it as needed. It is not at all difficult to soon acquire sufficient knowledge of the city to be able to move about without great loss of time. A street map is indispensable, and will greatly facilitate progress.

New York is a very cosmopolitan city. There is about it all the busy aspect which has often been described. The Broadway is frequently dangerously crowded with traffic, and the wonder is that, considering how badly lighted and paved is the city, more accidents do not occur. All know that New York is an island of itself, with one of the finest natural harbours in the world. It lies at the junction of the Hudson River and East River. This should aid largely in securing cleanliness and health to the city, but, on account of its most corrupt municipality, the streets are often in a dreadfully dirty condition, and the general sanitary arrangements are very ineffectual.

The city is not prolific in prominent and special sights, but among the first visits should be one to the Fifth-avenue. This is the finest fashionable street in America, and one of the handsomest in the world. Here the cream of New York society live. The largest of the houses in this street show to great advantage. The two recently built by Mr. Vanderbilt, situated at the corner of Fifty-fifth-street, are the most striking in the entire avenue; they are connected by a hall; one of them is inhabited by himself, and the other by a married daughter. In the interior furnishing of these more money has probably been lavished than in any other house of the same size in America. Not far from them is the house built by the late A. T. Stewart, which is a massive and striking structure. The evidences of wealth on every hand are apparent in this street; to rent a house in it is a certain passport to American society, and the houses in the side streets, all along the avenue, are also tenanted by well-to-do people. The churches of various denominations form a very prominent feature in this avenue; nearly every creed is represented, and some of their edifices are very fine, both in exterior and interior. The Presbyterian Church of Dr. John Hall is particularly so; this building cost, when completed, a million dollars, or £200,000. Those who take an interest in such buildings should not fail to pay this church a visit.

Central Park.—This is the greatest boast of the New Yorkers, and they have some reason to be proud of it. The ornamental gardening is one of the chief features, and it aids to make the park not only attractive but picturesque. The lakes in it cover 185 acres, and are supplied by the Croton Waterworks; pleasure boats of various sizes cover the water in the summer time, and with their little flags, and the awnings of the larger boats, help to make a pretty and effective sight. The trees in it are not remarkable either for size or variety, but what there are ornament delightful walks, winding in and out among the thickets, and providing a very pleasant shade in the summer time. The zoological houses of the American Museum of Natural History are not of the most comprehensive character, but contain some rare specimens. The best collection is the aviary, which has a selection of birds from almost every quarter of the world. The park, which is situated at the end of the Fifth-avenue, has cost, it is stated, ten million dollars, or £2,000,000, and the money has not been wasted, as has been the case with very nearly every public work in the city.

Commercial Buildings.—These of New York are among the sights of the city. The most prominent are the newspaper offices, such as *The Herald* and *The Tribune*; the offices of the Equitable Society, at Broadway and Cedar-street; and of the Mutual Company, Broadway and Liberty-street. " Business palaces" are numerous, and this is not to be wondered at, considering that the New Yorkers are above all things commercial. I need not enumerate them; Broadway, and some of the streets branching from it, contain many. In whatever business those may be who contemplate going out, they will be sure to find some commercial buildings which will be of special interest to them.

Public Buildings.—The chief among these may be mentioned:

The Post Office, which occupies the southern extremity of City Hall Park, opposite the Astor House. It is a most imposing building, in the Doric and Renaissance style of architecture, four stories in height, and with a peculiarly-constructed roof, surmounted by several Louvre domes. It has a frontage of 279ft. toward the park and 144ft. toward the south, and two equal façades of 262½ft. on Broadway and Park Row. The walls are of granite, and the entire cost of the building is stated as being between £1,200,000 and £1,400,000. It was completed seven years ago, and the interior arrangements cannot fail to strike the visitor.

City Hall—in City Hall Park.

New Court House, and other city buildings—in the same park.

City Prison, named the "Tombs"—in Centre-street.

Custom House and Sub-Treasury—Wall-street.

(Wall-street is the quarter for stockbrokers, and presents a lively appearance during the business part of the day).

Academy of Music—Fourteenth-street and Irving-place.

Academy of Designs—Twenty-third-street and Fourth-avenue.

Bible House—Eighth-street, Fourth-avenue.

Castle Garden—Battery Park, North River, the emigrant landing-place and departments.

Cooper Institute—junction of Third and Fourth Avenues.

Cotton Exchange—Hanover-square.

Christian Association Buildings — Twenty-third-street and Fourth-avenue.

Masonic Temple—corner of Twenty-third-street and Sixth-avenue.

Among the museums and libraries are:

The Lennox Library—near the Central Park.

UNION-SQUARE, NEW YORK.

Metropolitan Museum of Art—Fourteenth-street, near Sixth-avenue.

Astor Library—Lafayette-place.

Mercantile Library—for merchants and clerks. Astor-place.

Of theatres, New York has an ample supply. The chief are:

Wallack's—Thirtieth-street and Broadway.

Union-square—Fourteenth-street and Union-square.

Madison-square—West Twenty-fourth-street.

Haverley's—Fourteenth-street and Sixth-avenue.

Fifth-avenue—Twenty-eighth-street and Broadway.

Grand Opera House—Eighth-avenue and Twenty-third-street.

The most prominent squares are Mount Morris-square on the Fifth-avenue, between One Hundred and Twentieth-street and One Hundred and Twenty-fourth-street, embracing 20 acres; Madison-square, $6\frac{1}{2}$ acres in extent; Union-square, $3\frac{1}{2}$ acres (of this beautiful square the engraving on the preceding page conveys a good idea). The first of these comprises some very handsome buildings, and the last is filled with trees and has a large fountain in the centre. There are also here statues of Washington and Lincoln. Washington-square is in the west part of the city, in Fourth-street.

I may mention, with regard to the rates of admission to theatres, that for all parts of the house, half-a-dollar (two shillings) is charged, simply for entrance; the charges for a seat in addition range from half-a-dollar upwards. Do not buy tickets from speculators, who are outside every place of amusement.

I have already referred to the large number of churches—there being over 370 of all denominations in the city. The singing in most of them is quite a special feature, being usually rendered by professionals, who are liberally paid for their services.

Suburbs.—Brooklyn is to New York what the Surrey side is to London, and Birkenhead to Liverpool. It may be reached from any of the under-named ferries at the bottom of any of the following streets: Fulton, Wall, and Catherine Streets, and Peck

Slip. Fulton Ferry is the chief, and the horse cars going there are labelled "Fulton Ferries." The suspension bridge over the East River, from the New York to the Brooklyn side, is so gigantic a piece of engineering, that it has already ruined several firms, and it is impossible to say when it will be completed. Prospect Park is a very handsome public ground, which, Brooklynites say, surpasses the Central Park in New York. It has a lake, dairy cottage and barn, and a wide stretch of trees. Greenwood Cemetery should also be visited, being one of the largest burial-places on the globe. Costly monuments abound on every hand, and, aided by rising ground, with lakes and shady groves, a very picturesque scene is made up. The views from Ocean Hill and Battle Hill in the cemetery should not be missed. Brooklyn is said to be a city of churches. Here are the Tabernacle of Dr. Talmage and the Plymouth Church of the Rev. Henry Ward Beecher.

Short excursions may be made from New York to Coney Island, where is a fine sea beach, with capital bathing accommodation. This island may be reached from New York by Fulton Ferry, and by Smith and Jay-street horse cars, or by either of the horse-car lines to Greenwood, thence by the steam cars to the beach, or all the way by steamer from New York.

Rockaway Beach and Far Rockaway, both very picturesque lines of coast, are on the south side of Long Island. This district is always cool, even in the hottest weather. The sight of some thousand or more people, of either sex, bathing together *à la Français*, in the warmer months, will not be soon forgotten; and this sight, with the crowds of people on the beach partaking of shell-fish of every imaginable size and description, will be one long remembered. The beach has been celebrated by a popular song, commencing

> On old Long Island's sea-girt shore
> Many an hour I've whiled away,
> Listening to the breakers' roar
> That washed the beach of Rockaway.

Manhattan Beach is another pleasure resort, which should not on any account be missed. The monster hotel here will surprise many who come from Europe. Long Branch, on the New Jersey side, is a very enjoyable resort. It was here that the late President Garfield died. There is hotel accommodation for about forty thousand visitors, so that its popularity may be easily judged. The summer residences of many conspicuous Americans are here. Staten Island, the largest in the harbour, is very agreeable.

A visit should also be made to High Bridge, reached by a small steamer from Harlem, by Harlem River R.R., from Grand Central Depôt, or by carriage drive through the Central Park. The Croton Aqueduct crosses the Harlem River, and is a magnificent structure. It is built of granite, and spans the valley from cliff to cliff. It is 1450ft. long, and 114ft. high, supported on fourteen massive piers. At the south end of it is an immense reservoir, the water of which is pumped into it by special machinery.

CHAPTER VI.

UP THE HUDSON.

SOME of the prettiest scenery in America is to be found in the State of New York, and a more enjoyable trip cannot be had than one up the Hudson to Albany, or further north than this city if the tourist has time for it. Many enthusiastic writers about the River Hudson claim for it that, although it lacks the ruined castles which are to be found along the banks of the Rhine, and notwithstanding that the wild and romantic character of some of the Scotch lakes is also absent, yet the scenery along each side of it quite equals that of either. Every bend of the stream, after a certain point has been reached, reveals some new beauty, providing a rich variety of objects of interest. The river takes its rise in the Adirondack Mountains, in the northern part of the State. Unless the time of the visitor is more limited than the period named on the title-page of this book, it will be more enjoyable to journey to Albany the whole distance by the river. American steamboats are a sight in themselves, and their structure and general luxuriousness will be matters of attractiveness to the tourist the first time he steps on one, which may probably be in taking the short trip now indicated.

The morning boats leave New York at an early hour, but there is also an afternoon boat. On all there is ample accommodation for dining and sleeping. The chief points of interest begin after arriving at West Point, which is a journey by rail (Hudson River Railway) of from two to four hours. The first stopping place of prominence is Westchester, where many New York merchants reside, in villas that will at once strike the visitor for their variety in styles of architecture and building materials. On the western side of the river, after passing Spuytenduyvel, and at Fort Lee begin the Palisades. This is the term applied to immense masses of rock rising perpendicularly out of the water, and that extend in one unbroken line for more than twenty miles; this wall of rock rises in many places to the height of 300ft., but for the greater part of the distance the height is lower and more uniform. The summit of these cliffs is thickly wooded, and until a few years ago no sign of habitation could be noticed on the top of them. Now a large hotel indicates life and civilisation, and this crowns one of the taller rocks; pretty villas have also been erected. The Palisades are narrow, being in some places not more than three-quarters of a mile wide, the top being singularly level, and affording a long narrow tableland. During the heat of summer these rocks afford a delightfully cool place, where long rambles may be taken on the level surface in the pleasant shade of the trees.

Tarrytown, the next place, is where Washington Irving resided. This name, he says, was given in former times by the housewives of the neighbouring country, in consequence of the inveterate propensity of their husbands to linger about the village taverns on market days. Sing Sing, the State prison, is also near here.

The next stopping place of interest is Peekskill, and after leaving here the Highlands of the Hudson are entered. These present a continual change of rich scenery.

West Point is the next stopping place of importance. Here are the Military Academy Docks. The military school is one of the first of its kind in America. The cadets' parade, morning and evening, is quite a sight. After leaving West Point, the Storm King, the largest hill of the range, is seen, and on the opposite side is Cornwall Landing, round about which there is some admirable scenery. Newburgh comes next, which shows all the life of a large trade. On the bluffs below it were Washington's head-quarters, and other reminders are present of the struggle of a hundred years ago.

Poughkeepsie follows, and it is from this place that the greatest beauty of the river scenery commences. Near it is Vassar College, where from three to four hundred young ladies live for a few years an academic life, with examinations as severe as at Harvard, Yale, or other universities for the sterner sex. The college stands in its own grounds, which cover some two hundred acres. After leaving Poughkeepsie, the Catskill Mountains, which can be seen for a very long distance from the river, begin now to assume a nobler aspect, and form a striking background to the beautiful scenery stretching from them to the riverside. Catskill Station is the landing place for the mountains, for those who desire to remain for a time in this delightful spot. Here there are always stage coaches waiting, which will convey the tourists through Sleepy Hollow, where Rip Van Winkle is fabled to have had his long, deep sleep. All along here are districts patronised largely by holiday people from the various cities of the State. The remaining part of the journey, from Catskill to Albany, can either be performed by the boat or by rail. Albany is the capital of the State of New York. It is very picturesquely situated, and now a flourishing city, with a large and increasing trade. Eight railways terminate in or pass through it. Within easy distance are several thriving villages, one of which—Lebanon—is the chief centre of the Shaker community, with their peculiar forms of worship. Troy is eight miles only from Albany, with a choice of reaching it by street car, omnibus, or railway. This is quite a flourishing town; a variety of trades are carried on, and it possesses also some of the most extensive lumber and timber depôts of the world.

Glen Falls and Saratoga Springs are well deserving of a visit if the tourist has time for it. These places lie conveniently north of Albany, but I would remind the reader that Saratoga has the reputation of being excessively dear. It affords, however, a capital idea of what a fashionable season resort is like in America.

Before taking this trip up the Hudson, the tourist should decide whether he will come back to New York or go on to Boston by rail, which can easily be done. There are two lines of steamers that go up and down the Hudson—the New Jersey Steamboat Company, or the People's Line, and the Troy Steamboat Company. If time is very limited, take train by the New York Central and Hudson River Railroad for West Point or Poughkeepsie, and proceed thence to Albany by boat. This, however, must all depend on what leisure there may be at disposal.

The fare from New York to Albany is 2dols. (8s.), and the time occupied about ten hours for the whole distance of 148 miles. The journey by rail takes five hours, and the fare is 3dols. 10c. (12s. 5d.). The hotels at the latter place are the Stanwix Hall and the Delavan and Congress Hall, at 3dols. per day. The journey by rail from Albany to Boston occupies about six hours.

As a special object of interest at Albany, I may name the New Capitol, which was commenced in 1871. It is claimed to be the largest and most splendid edifice in America, next to the Capitol at Washington. The style is Renaissance, and the chief material Maine granite. State-street contains State Hall, the State Library, with its 86,000 volumes, and an interesting collection of curiosities and historical relics, including Washington's dress sword and pistol.

Should the tourist return to New York and then purpose leaving for Boston, the best route to select is the Fall River Line. Sometimes, in the season, there is some very brisk competition among the companies for this traffic. The usual fare is 5dols., but it often comes down to 3dols.

CHAPTER VII.

BOSTON.

I HAVE already mentioned that it was optional whether the tourist went direct to Boston from Albany or returned to New York, proceeding afterwards to the first-named city. Adopting the latter plan, one of several available routes can be selected. For variety in travel, the Fall River route is preferable, being partially by land and partially by water. The steamers running on the river would afford a further opportunity of observing to what a high state of perfection the Americans have brought river travelling. These powerful and peculiarly-constructed boats are different from those in use in any other country in the world, except the adjoining Dominion of Canada. The only fault, to a nervous traveller, perhaps, is that they go too fast, and that they steam at times dangerously near each other, but this is a matter to which the tourist will soon become well accustomed. If the rail journey is preferred for the whole distance, there is a good train leaves New York at 11.35 p.m., due in Boston the next morning at 7.55 a.m. The fare is 5dols., Pullman sleeping car extra; this is by the New York and New England Railroad from the Grand Central Depôt. The Fall River line takes about three hours longer, the fare being 4dols., or 16s. The leading sights by this route are the Penal and Benevolent institutions on Blackwell's Island, Randall's Island, and Ward's Island. "Hell Gate" is not an attractive name or place, but its rocky dangers account, perhaps, for its designation. These and other chief points of interest will be passed in the evening, the boat leaving at 4.0 or 5.0 p.m., according to the season; the remainder of the water journey affords few attractions.

Those interested in colleges and similar buildings would be sure to select the rail route in order to pass through New Haven, the largest city in Connecticut. Its origin dates back to 1638. Here is Yale College, founded in 1700; besides its academic department, the college has a law school, a medical school, a scientific school, a theological school, and a school of fine arts. The library, a very handsome building, has about 100,000 volumes. In the art building are valuable collections of historical paintings, Italian pictures, and casts from Greek antiquities. The entire buildings are most interesting.

The available hotels are the St. James's, United States, and Rivere House, at 3dols. per day, or, in the latter case, more, according to the location of the bedroom. The Maverick Hotel, Maverick-square, East Boston, is another house which may be named, but, on account of having to cross the ferry to and from Boston proper, some inconvenience would probably be experienced.

Of the two cities, Boston is better paved and lighted than New York. It is the capital of Massachusetts, and the Bostonians claim that it is the intellectual metropolis of the New World. The Boston merchants are said to be the most enterprising in all the States, the "drummers" (or travellers) the boldest, and the ladies the prettiest. How far this is true is not for me to "guess;" the tourist must judge for himself, and he will, doubtless, have good opportunity for doing so. Boston and Philadelphia are much more representative of Trans-Atlantic towns than is cosmopolitan New York. Most English visitors would very soon find themselves at home, so genial and hospitable are the Bostonians; and in no part of the States is the feeling towards England and Englishmen so warm and genuine as it is found in this city. The streets are, as I have said, better paved than those in New York, but they are much more irregular, and are not laid out at right angles. There is, in fact, an old-standing joke that "they were laid out by the cows going to pasture." It is as easy to get lost in its winding thoroughfares as it is in Chester or Bristol. In addition to these features Boston possesses several buildings of historical interest, the chief of which is the Old State House, erected in 1748, and used for many years as the head-quarters of the State Legislature. Faneuil Hall is another building of more than ordinary interest. It is situated in a square, bearing its name, but the hall itself is best known as the "Cradle of Liberty." It was erected in 1742, by an old Huguenot merchant, and contains some national pictures illustrative of scenes of the early struggles of the patriots for independence. Fire destroying it, it was rebuilt in 1761, and for some time prior to 1776 it served as a barracks for the British troops. General Washington entered the city, and the troops of George the Third were sent to the rightabout. Whenever any great question, political or social, is to be discussed by the Bostonians, this is their place of meeting. No money is ever allowed to be taken at the door, and an old charter forbids the sale or lease of this historic edifice.

Fortunately for the reputation of the Boston hackmen, the fares here are more reasonable than is the case in New York. For one passenger per course in the city proper, one dollar; and each additional passenger, 50 cents; from midnight until 6 a.m., double the above fares.

Other antiquities are "Brattle-street Church," with one of the round shot still embedded in the front wall as a memento of the Charlestown bombardment during the War of Independence; "Ordway Hall," in Province Court House, which was once the residence of the colonial governors; and "Liberty Tree," on Boston Common, with a history dating back to Puritan times, and often the scene now of many patriotic gatherings. Of this common the Bostonians are as proud as Londoners are of any of their parks. It is triangular in shape, and covers nearly fifty acres. It is beautifully shaded with stately elms, and has about it a homely charm, which makes the New Englanders rejoice in it. Adjoining the common are the "Public Gardens," in which there is a small but very pretty lake, derisively called the "Frog Pond."

COMMONWEALTH-AVENUE, BOSTON.

The ornamental gardening in these grounds and the equestrian statue of Washington are especially to be noticed.

The most prominent streets are "Washington," as a commercial street; "Beacon" and "Tremont" Streets, as fashionable thoroughfares, where milliners and tailors largely congregate;

"State," "Congress," and other streets branching from the Old Court House, for insurance, financial, law, and similar offices. Around the common are also a number of other fashionable streets which will interest the visitor. "Bunker's Hill Monument," on Breed's Hill, is a spot to be early visited as the birthplace of American National Independence. It is a high and massive tower, built square, and

CITY HALL, BOSTON.

from its summit can be obtained an excellent view of the whole city and country for miles round. It is a stiff climb up, but certainly worth the labour.

There are many beautiful avenues, of which Commonwealth-avenue is perhaps the finest. It is 240ft. wide, and through the centre runs a long park, with rows of trees, as will be seen from the illustration given on page 46.

Among the chief public buildings may be named the Public

Free Library, a very fair indication, with its several branches, of the intellectual status of the Bostonians; and the Custom House, Exchange, and Post Office, in State-street. In School-street is the City Hall, of which an engraving is shown on page 47. It is built of white Concord granite, in the Italian Renaissance style, and is surmounted by a Louvre dome 109ft. high; the total cost of it was over £100,000. Opposite this is an immense statue of Franklin. The general and city hospitals may likewise be mentioned. The various bridges connecting the suburbs with the city proper are noticeable. The suburbs are—Cambridge on the west, Charlestown on the north, and Chelsea and East Boston on the east. It will be remembered that Charlestown Harbour played an important part in the Civil War.

Another place of interest is the Museum of Fine Arts, in Art-square, which is an elegant building, richly adorned with terra-cotta bas-reliefs, copings, and mouldings. The picture galleries here contain as good and valuable a selection as will be found in the States. Of public libraries Boston can claim to have an exceptionally large number. The Free Library named above has over 260,000 volumes, besides 100,000 pamphlets, and a collection of engravings. The Athenæum, an imposing edifice in the Palladian style, has 96,000 volumes in its library. The Academy of Arts and Sciences, in the same buildings, has a library of over 15,000 volumes.

The harbour of Boston is one of the best and most spacious on the coast. Frequent excursions to different points take place during the summer season, and, by taking a steamer to Hingham, from Liverpool Wharf, the principal islands (some of them very pretty), and also the fortifications, may be seen.

Plymouth is only a short distance from Boston, and should be visited. Here the Pilgrim Fathers landed in 1620, in the "Mayflower." In every period of American history the character of the descendants of these families, who sought in a new country freedom from the persecution which had driven them from their native land, has been stamped on the New Englanders. They have been foremost in adherence to principles in every national struggle which the country has passed through. They were the first to take the lead in the revolutionary contest against the mother country, over a hundred years ago, and in the Civil War they were foremost to assert the rights of the slave, and to find the sinews of War for that gigantic struggle. At Plymouth is the monument showing the landing place of our countrymen; and Pilgrim's Hall, in which are a number of "Mayflower" relics, will be of interest to all who visit the place.

Cambridge, a suburb, as stated, should not be neglected. The tramway runs the whole distance, about three miles from the city. The residence of the late Henry Wadsworth Longfellow will be shown by the tram conductor. This house was formerly the headquarters of Washington, and so, on this account, has a double interest. With the freedom which characterises all things American, it is usual for visitors, even if they have not an introduction to the house, to enter and walk round the grounds. It is a very picturesque spot, and I shall not readily forget my saunter there a few years ago, when I was fortunate in having the only sight I ever had of the great poet. The chief buildings at Cambridge are those of Harvard University, comprising altogether some fifteen to twenty different structures. If the college is in session, the interest attaching to the visit will be greatly enhanced. The Anatomical Museum and the Observatory are special objects to be visited. Near at hand, also, is the tree under which Washington took command of the American forces. It is around Harvard and Yale College, in Connecticut, that much of the intellectual life of the States centres. It has been my good fortune to meet not a few students who have passed through one or the other, and also professors, and from facts gathered from these gentlemen I think their whole system of training has much to recommend it.

There will be no difficulty in seeing over, at any reasonable hour, some of the buildings. Mount Auburn Cemetery, about four miles from the city, and Wenham Lake, which largely supplies Europe with ice, should be also seen.

Concord is a pretty little town on the Concord branch of the Merrimac River, where lived Nathaniel Hawthorne, Ralph Waldo Emerson, and other celebrities who have passed away, and where to-day reside Mrs. Harriet Beecher Stowe and Mr. Charles W. Clemence, better known as "Mark Twain."

Lynn is within easy distance, too, of Boston. This is the seat of American shoe manufacturing, and gives one a capital idea of an industrial centre on the other side of the Atlantic.

CHAPTER VIII.

MONTREAL.

As the natural wish of all making a first visit to the United States would be to see Niagara Falls, I would suggest that, instead of going direct to there from Boston or New York, they should travel first to Montreal. This, with a visit to Toronto, within easy distance of the Falls, and one or two other cities, would enable the tourist to have a brief but very interesting sight of a portion of Canada, which could not fail to greatly enhance the pleasure of the tour.

There is a choice of several routes, the distance varying according to that selected. It can be reached by the Lowell and Vermont Central Railroad, the distance being 334 miles; or *viâ* Fitchburg and Rutland, 344 miles; or through Portland by the Boston and Maine Railroad, which joins with the Grand Trunk Line of Canada, and so has direct communication with Montreal. There is the choice of a good train which leaves Boston at 5.0 p.m. in the evening, due in Montreal at about 8.0 a.m. the following morning, or a day train leaving at about 8.0 a.m., and occupying fourteen hours on the journey. The first-class fare is about 8dols., or 32s.

The chief points of interest on the route are Lawrence, noted for its cotton and print manufactories, which lie scattered along the banks of the Merrimac River. These mills, with those at Manchester and Lowell, are the largest in the States in these industries—the district is, in fact, the Lancashire of America—

and for cleanliness and conveniently-arranged manufacturing centres, they convey a very favourable impression. Anyone interested in these important trades would not pass through the districts named without remaining for a day or so to go over some of the mills—a privilege which it is not by any means difficult to obtain.

Exeter, lying on Exeter River, has a good coasting trade and several important factories. Newmarket Junction connects with Concord, or direct on to Portsmouth on the Piscatagua River. There is a good harbour here, and it is also the seat of one of the United States Navy Yards.

Portland is a flourishing commercial city, lying on a peninsula at the south-west of Casco Bay. Since a large fire, which occurred in this town in 1866, its newly-built streets have a striking and attractive appearance. Congress-street is the most important business thoroughfare of the town. The prominent buildings are the City Hall, Court House, and Marine Hospital. A capital view of the White Mountains can be obtained from the Observatory, which overlooks the harbour. Between Portland and Montreal there is not much of special interest, and unless the time at the disposal of the tourist is longer than six weeks, and there are points which he desires to explore, such as the White Mountains and other places, I would counsel a direct journeying from Boston to Montreal.

The Victoria Bridge, across the River St. Lawrence, which is nearly two miles long, cost, it is said, considerably over a million pounds to build. It is in tubular form, on the same plan as the Menai Bridge, on twenty-three spans of 242ft. each, with a centre one of 330ft. The late Robert Stephenson was its chief constructor, and it was opened by the Prince of Wales in 1860.

The hotels in Montreal are numerous, and the number of representatives of these generally present at the depôt on the arrival of the trains is rather bewildering. The comical manner

MONTREAL, FROM THE ST. LAWRENCE.

in which they call out, one after the other, the names of their respective hotels is very amusing. Of this elaborate choice, selection may be made of the St. Lawrence Hall, or the Windsor Hotel, the best of the two, at 3dols., or 12s. 6d., per day, American plan. There are also a number of *cafés* and boarding houses on a smaller scale. Good accommodation can be obtained at some of these for 2dols. per day. The use of the omnibus from the depôt to the hotel will be put down in the bill at 2s., or even a dollar if there is much luggage.

The view of Montreal from the terminus of the Grand Trunk Railway is very disappointing, but when the city is explored and its different points of interest visited, this feeling invariably gives place to one of admiration. The illustration on the preceding page gives a good view of the city from the River St. Lawrence. The visitor will, by the time that he reaches the capital of the Canadian Dominion, have become accustomed to the wooden pavements; these, in the hot months of the year, become so heated that they are somewhat uncomfortable to walk upon.

Montreal conveys a very good idea of the progress which Canada has made during, say, the last twenty-five years. It is the largest and most prosperous of the cities in British North America. There are many Americans who argue that Canada certainly has not progressed with the rapidity which has characterised the States. Whether this is so or not it can scarcely form part of our present work to inquire into, but my own conviction is that the leading cities of Canada will compare very favourably with the cities of the States. I may mention, in passing, that one reason given for the slow rate of progress which Canada can claim for herself, is that her population has in it a strong French element, who, it is asserted, do not make the most enterprising colonists. In Montreal alone there are some 20,000, principally engaged as work-people in the lighter trades, such as the making up of millinery, clothing, and fur caps. The

Catholic Cathedral of Notre Dame, standing in the Place d'Armes in the street bearing the name of the church, and which comfortably holds 10,000 people, is an evidence of the French prominence in the population. This is a fine building, Gothic in style, with two tall towers, from the tops of which there is a magnificent view of the city and its precincts, which should not be missed. The River St. Lawrence lies at the foot of the city, and on the rapidly rising ground from the river a large number of new and costly residences have been built, which convey a very good idea of Montreal's commercial prosperity. These houses are built chiefly of greyish limestone from adjacent quarries; and, with its tall spires and glittering roofs and domes, and the beautiful villas that stud its lofty background of Mount Royal, the city presents as attractive and picturesque a panorama as can be found in any part of Canada or the States. Mount Royal will repay the tourist for the rather arduous climb up to its summit. Very pleasantly cool in August is the top of this elevated ground, and a number of pretty little villas of wood, scattered all about, betoken how many of the well-to-do citizens of Montreal reside there.

The public and commercial buildings of the city are numerous. Among these the City Hall is the most prominent, and, as a municipal building, will compare very favourably with many on this side of the Atlantic. Others are the Court House; the Bank of Montreal, near the Cathedral; the McGill College, at the foot of Mount Royal; Bonsecours Market, on the quay, which has a large dome and capital internal arrangements; and St. Patrick's Hall, in Victoria-square. The handsome Nelson Monument will also be noticed. Of churches and chapels there is ample choice, and some of these, for chasteness in style of architecture and for interior fittings, would very suitably afford models for such buildings in this country. The chief commercial thoroughfare is St. Paul-street, and Notre Dame and Great St. James Streets are noted for extensive shops, or "stores," to use the trans-Atlantic phrase. The fine quays along the river present, during seven or eight months of the year, a lively scene of excitement in the coming and going of large and small steamers. As two additional attractions, I may mention that the church of the Jesuits contains a good collection of pictures by the old masters, and one of three nunneries may be visited at certain seasons of the year if the visitor has any desire to do so. Many excursions of interest can be made from Montreal, but the most indispensable, and what would to many be the gem of the whole tour, would be a sail up the Lachine Rapids, which should on no account be missed by the visitor. For the benefit of those who may not have an opportunity of "shooting the rapids" for themselves, the description given in the following chapter will be of interest.

CHAPTER IX.

SHOOTING THE RAPIDS.

"SHOOTING the rapids" means everything that this rather startling title indicates. Shooting a river weir is a pastime sometimes resorted to, but that bears about as much resemblance to shooting the rapids as bathing in a ten-inch water bucket does to a splash in a large swimming bath. There is no occasion to understand from this that it is a piece of bravery on the part of the person who pays his fare to undergo the operation. Not a bit of it. You keep your seat or walk about, in a good-sized steamer which does the "shooting" business, the care and responsibility of which steamer and passengers lie in the hands of the man at the wheel and the pilot. Personally, I would rather be a "sandwich man" walking between two advertising boards, navigating the Strand on a windy day, than I would be either a pilot or a helmsman on board one of those steamers.

I left Montreal about four in the afternoon by one of the steam-cars of the Grand Trunk Railway, and travelled down to Lachine. The line runs almost parallel with the River St. Lawrence the whole distance, and is dotted with numerous pretty villa residences, built of wood in the orthodox style of Canadian architecture. As well as owning some 2500 miles of track, the Grand Trunk Railway Company are also the proprietors of a number of steamers which ply on the river. These steamers are not as large as those sailing between Birkenhead and

Liverpool, although larger than those on the Thames, nor do they vie in interior accommodation with the splendid vessels of the Cunard Company, but are, nevertheless, luxuriously fitted up. They are used, I may incidentally remark, very extensively by the Canadians for picnics; and a day's sail in one of them down to the Thousand Islands—another trip which should be made by the tourist if he has time—costs only 5s. each person, exclusive of meals. The fare for the round trip—that is, to Lachine by rail and back by steamer — costs only 2s., first class.

The Lachine Rapids are between seven and eight miles west of Montreal, and are the most dangerous of a succession of rapids in the St. Lawrence River. Steamers, however, descend them in safety, but smaller craft would speedily come to grief. Although the passage of the rapids is dangerous, a sense of pleasurable excitement takes the place of timidity in the minds of tourists in general. The pilot is insensible to fear, though not to the responsibility which rests upon him. Accidents have occurred, but not for some years.

I took my seat in the bow of the steamer, and waited expectantly for the approaching of the rapids. We steamed on for a considerable distance before any perceptible difference in the water could be noticed. A portion of the river was passed in which scarcely a ripple could be discerned, and I learned afterwards that this is one of the deepest parts of the St. Lawrence. The width at this place is about four miles. Away we steamed, and a gurgling of the water could now be easily seen. This gradually increased, until we reached a spot where the water was dashing in tons over massive rocks, just between two of which our boat sailed. The noise of the water grew greater as we progressed, until the whole of that around the boat became furiously restless. Two men were now at the helm, and the pilot did not move his eyes off one particular spot. On we sped, and the water boiled around us as if a very Nebuchadnezzar's furnace were below it. The spray was dashed upwards for a score of feet, and the steamer began to pitch in a frantic manner. The force of the water against the sides of the vessel was simply terrible. A thought flashed through my mind: Suppose the chains of the rudder should snap—what then? I could imagine no one escaping, except by a miracle, from those rolling, tumbling, maddened waves, dashing headlong over gigantic rocks of a thousand years' standing. One moment we were on the top of a wave, and below we could see the deep trough, with the water running hither and thither, searching, as it were, for a quiet resting place and failing to find it. The whole waves appeared in a state of civil war. Half the water is American and the other half British, and there was every resemblance of war to the knife. The river was as varied in its colour as it was in the direction of its currents. One narrow strip just beneath our bow was as black as midnight, and a little way from our boat was a track of bright blue. These and other colours, fringed with white foam, made a picture in my mind which will never fade away. I would willingly go all the distance from London to Canada to spend another hour on those rapids. During the most dangerous and the most interesting portion of them, I was not conscious of taking breath. I do not remember hearing a single word spoken by anyone for at least ten minutes. All appeared to be under the spell of an excitement, intense and enjoyable. We left the rapids at last by a very sudden turn of the boat, and I could not suppress the wish to see us wheel round and try the journey the other way. But such desire was of no avail, as we were rapidly nearing Montreal. Even very timid people feel heedless of the danger, but I am sure that the heedlessness arises from a sense of confidence in the steamer and its officers. You know, or probably learn, that all the officials are doing that sort of thing every day when the river is navigable. Nevertheless, we felt a considerable amount of admiration for the pilot. As we steamed towards Montreal he took the trouble to point out to me the prominent public buildings; he also told me that he had been a pilot on the St. Lawrence for over ten years, and gave me other particulars of his history. A few days afterwards I stood *by* the Niagara Falls, but previously I was *on* the rapids, and perhaps that is the reason why I experienced more pleasure in the one case than the other. I was awed with Niagara, but I experienced sensations of a different nature when "shooting the rapids."

CHAPTER X.

QUEBEC AND OTTAWA.

A VISIT to Quebec must be quite optional with the visitor if he desires to be home again within a limited time. Personally, I did not visit this city on the occasion of my first crossing the Atlantic for a six weeks' holiday. It could, however, be included in a tour extending over this period, as it is only an eight hours' journey from Montreal, the distance being 178 miles by the Grand Trunk Railway. If the time of the year is favourable, it is by far the preferable plan to go by steamer up the St. Lawrence, the distance being 260 miles. The fare is usually, for first class, including state rooms and meals, 3dols. (12s.), and, second class, without meals, as low as 4s. The fare is considerably higher by rail.

As I have already remarked, there is at times considerable variation in fares, especially where there is competition, so that the fares I name must be accepted as approximate rather than the exact amount.

The river journey is cheap, as will be seen, and affords views of as fine scenery as could be wished for. Quebec has been called the "Gibraltar of America," on account of the extensive fortifications of the "Citadel," which occupy some forty acres, and are considered to be impregnable. It is the oldest city after Montreal, and becomes of increasing importance each year, not only for its lumber and timber markets, but for its general maritime trade. Boots and shoes, furniture, and machinery are also manufactured largely in Quebec. The city is divided into the Upper and Lower Town, the descent from the latter to the Upper Town being by Mountain-street—a very appropriate name, for it is a steep and winding thoroughfare. The Lower Town represents the commercial part of the city, and is built around the base of the promontory. The most conspicuous buildings of the Upper Town proper are the Seminary and Laval University, the Ursulines, and the Hospital or Hôtel Dieu. There is also here a Jesuit College, which was founded as far back as 1633, but was after 1812 occupied as a barracks. St. Louis and St. John are very pretty suburbs of the Upper City, and contain a large number of private residences. Here also are several conventual establishments and churches. A labyrinth of irregular streets make up the busiest part of the Lower Town. St. Paul-street stretches westward on the narrow strand between the cliff and the bay, and contains many manufactories and other commercial establishments.

The hotels are: St. Louis, in St. Louis-street, near Durham-terrace, and the Russell House, corner of Ann and Garden Streets; from 3dols. to 4dols. per day.

The Plains of Abraham are reached *viâ* the St. Louis Gate. Here Wolfe, the English general, fell in the memorable battle of 13th September, 1759, and a column of not large proportions has been erected to his memory.

From Quebec, several interesting excursions may be made. The Isle of Orleans, by ferry-boat; the Falls of Montmorenci, eight miles below Quebec; other falls are Chaudière, eighteen miles from the city, which are reached *viâ* Point Levi, on the opposite side of the St. Lawrence. Here the river plunges in a sheet 350ft. wide over a precipice 150ft. high, and presents a very striking sight.

Even a very brief visit to the Dominion would, of course, be very incomplete if Ottawa, the seat of Government and where the Governor-General resides, were not seen. It may be reached from Montreal up the Ottawa River, the distance being 100 miles, or viâ Grand Trunk Railway to Prescott Junction, and then viâ St. Lawrence and Ottawa R.R., 170 miles.

The Russell House, Daniels' and the Albion Hotels, may be mentioned. Charges, 2dols. 50c. to 3dols. 50c. per day.

Ottawa is divided into the Upper and the Lower Town by the Rideau Canal, which passes through it and connects it with Kingston on Lake Ontario. Within the city proper two bridges span the river, one of stone and the other of stone and iron, and it has eight very large locks. Outside the city precincts there are also bridges connecting Ottawa with the suburban towns of Hull and New Edinburgh, districts very picturesque certainly, but widely different from the towns on this side of the Atlantic from which they take their names. The majority of the streets are wide and regular, and present during the day, especially when the Dominion Parliament is sitting, a very busy aspect. Sparks and Sussex Streets are among the most prominent.

The population of the capital is rapidly increasing. Anyone interested in the timber trade may have an opportunity of witnessing, in the immediate neighbourhood of the city, the most extensive operations in the rafting and sawing of lumber and pine of any district in the whole range of the continent. Flour mills, foundries, and engineering works are to be found in considerable number and size.

The points of attraction, of course, in the city are the Parliament House and Government buildings. They form three sides of a very large quadrangle on Barrack Hill, some 150ft. above the river. Parliament House forms the south side of the quadrangle, and is 472ft. long and 572ft. deep from the front of the main tower to the rear of the library. The central tower is 180ft. high, and the body of the building 40ft. high. The departmental buildings are on the north of Parliament House, and form the east and west sides of the quadrangle. The eastern block is 318ft. long by 253ft. deep, and the western

211ft. long by 277ft. deep. Here are the Post Office, model department of the Patent Office, and various Government offices. The buildings cost a total sum of 4,000,000 dols., or £800,000, and are constructed in the Italian-Gothic style, of cream-coloured sandstone—a native stone found in large quantities in the Dominion. The roofs are covered with green and purple slates, and the pinnacles are ornamented with iron, relieved with various coloured paints. The Senate Hall is close by the main entrance; it is luxuriously furnished and capacious. The viceregal canopy and throne are at one end of this hall, and at the other end are a marble statue and a portrait of Queen Victoria, together with full-length portraits, painted by Sir Joshua Reynolds, of George III. and Queen Charlotte. The Chamber of Commons is on the left of the entrance hall, and contains some beautiful marble columns and arches. In the library are about 45,000 volumes. The quadrangle has a very pretty appearance, it being laid out with trees and flowers. Should the House be in session at the time of the visit, there would be no difficulty in obtaining admission to the galleries. Often the presenting of a card to the doorkeeper will secure it. Rideau Hall, the official residence of the Governor-General, the Marquis of Lorne, is in New Edinburgh, across the Ottawa River, and is a very fashionable district. Students of colonial architecture will have much in this district to gratify their curiosity.

Notre Dame, the Roman Catholic cathedral, is a very handsome building. It has double spires, 200ft. high. There is a painting, said to be by Murillo, "The Flight into Egypt." The buildings of the Ladies' College are also worth noting. The falls of the river will be a source of great interest to the visitor. Chaudière Falls are 40ft. high, and over 200ft. wide; they are near the centre of the river, and have many features of grandeur. The water of the Chaudière (or cauldron) Great Falls is very deep, the sounding line not having found a bottom at 300ft. Below these falls there is a splendid suspension bridge, from which a capital view can be obtained. The Little Chaudière Falls are a mile from Ottawa, and are eclipsed by those within the precincts of the city. Rideau Falls and De Cheyne Rapids, the latter about eight miles from Ottawa, are worth a visit if the tourist is so disposed. The timber "shoots," running alongside the falls, convey a capital idea of the immensity of the Canadian lumber trade.

CHAPTER XI.

TORONTO.

THE distance from Montreal to Toronto is 333 miles by Grand Trunk Railway, or the whole distance can be made by steamer, on the River St. Lawrence and Lake Ontario, if the visitor has inclination and time; and the sail is a most enjoyable one. Toronto is a typical Canadian city. It is situated on a bay of Lake Ontario, and presents, with its lake trade, a thriving aspect. It was founded in 1794; and, in passing, I may say that "Toronto" means, in the language of the North American Indians, "the place of meeting." There are many commercial buildings of interest in the leading thoroughfares of King and Yonge-streets. The latter street extends through a flourishing agricultural district to Lake Simcoe, which is thirty-six miles distant from the city, and affords an unbroken drive the entire distance.

The University of Toronto is a splendid structure, standing in a large park, and approached by an avenue half-a-mile long, lined with double rows of fine trees. The college was founded fifty-five years ago, and has a liberal endowment. Access to the main portions of the buildings is easy. Knox College, a Presbyterian institution, is a prominent pile of buildings, near the university just named. The Post Office, the City Hall in Front-street, near Lake Shore, Lawrence Market, Custom House, Osgood Hall, and Merchants' Exchange, should all be visited. Osgood Hall, in Queen-street, is an imposing building of the

Ionic order, and contains the provincial law courts and a large law library.

The (Episcopal) Cathedral of St. James, corner of King-street, is a very handsome building, in the Gothic style of the thirteenth century. Some of the prettiest churches and chapels in the entire Dominion are to be found in Toronto. The Normal School, the Model Schools, the Educational Museum, Trinity College, the General Hospital, and the Crystal Palace, in which are held annual exhibitions of the products of the province, are all objects of interest.

The Queen's Park covers about fifty acres, and is very skilfully laid out and well shaded with trees. There is a monument in it, erected to the memory of the Canadians who fell in repelling the Fenian invasion of 1866.

There is usually some good sculling on the lake that will to some be an attraction. It is here that Hanlan won his laurels, the lake having afforded him one of the best practice-grounds in the world.

The hotels are Rossin House, 2dols. to 3dols. per day; Queen's Hotel, 3dols.; Revere House, 2dols.

I may here state that, with regard to trade and navigation, the returns for the year ending June, 1882, show the very favourable condition of Canada. The exports and imports have been steadily increasing during the past few years:

	Exports.	Imports.
1878-79	£14,298,251	£16,392,885
1879-80	17,582,291	17,297,949
1880-81	19,658,164	21,066,188
1881-82	20,427,440	23,883,900

It is not uninteresting to notice the growth of imports from Great Britain, which, contrary to expectation in many quarters, have largely increased, tending to show that up to the present time, at any rate, the tariff has not adversely affected such importations. In 1879 the value of these imports was £6,198,626, and in 1882 £10,119,460. The values of goods imported from the United States during the same periods were £8,749,844 and £9,657,810 respectively, showing an increase of only £910,000, as against the increase of nearly £4,000,000 in British importations.

CHAPTER XII.

THE NIAGARA FALLS.

THE next point of interest, after leaving Toronto, is Niagara Falls, and naturally a first visit to this celebrated spot will be eagerly looked forward to. The journey to the Falls from Toronto occupies about two hours. An hour-and-a-quarter are taken up in crossing Lake Ontario and in the remainder of the journey by rail to the village or town of Niagara Falls. Before reaching the American side of the lake General Brock's monument (who fell here in 1812) will be noticed on the Canadian side, and immediately opposite, on the other side, is the United States battery. The eddying of the stream, caused by the rush of water over the Falls, will be noticed here, although they are four miles away.

I received, prior to visiting the Falls, various pieces of advice about the exorbitant prices which are charged at the hotels and for everything bought in the district. "Do not buy anything, not even a hasty lunch, within three miles of the Falls," said a Montreal tradesman to me. "You will, of course, 'do' Niagara," wrote a friend to me, before I sailed on my first visit, "and take precious good care not to be done by the score or more cheate there are at that greatly visited spot;" and so, in many respects, the idea has got abroad that Niagara is the most expensive place to visit of any resort in the States. To the credit of Niagara, it may be said that it is no dearer place than Brighton, Buxton, or the English or Scotch lakes in the season.

So much has been said and written of the Falls that the subject is thoroughly threadbare, and I feel somewhat disposed to say, as another writer has done : " There are some waterfalls hereabouts which are said to be very pretty. For a description of them the reader is referred to the works of the late Mr. Charles Dickens, Dr. Charles Mackay, Mr. Nicholas Woods, Mr. N. P. Willis, Baron Humboldt, Sir Charles Lyell, Professor Agassiz, and ten thousand more or less accomplished tourists, *savans*, and sketch writers." With this in mind, the little I have to say will be trite and matter-of-fact.

Where there is occasion to remain all night, the available hotels are the International, at 3dols. a day, on the American side, and on the Canadian side the Clifton House, at the same tariff. When time is short, by leaving Toronto early in the day, opportunity will be given to see the Falls and pass on in the evening to the next stopping place.

It is a very general but a very true expression, with regard to the Falls, that the impression on first glancing at them is one of keen disappointment. The spot has been so eulogised by poets and prose writers that a picture of vastness and immensity takes possession of the imagination respecting them, and yet the most elaborate description must fail to picture the scene as it actually appears. It is one of those things which must indeed " be seen to be appreciated." An honest Hibernian, while he gazed upon it, being asked if it was not the most wonderful thing that he had ever seen, replied : " Never a bit, man, never a bit. Shure, it's no wonder at all that the wather should fall down there, for I would like to know what could hinther it ; but its mighty quare, though, I'm thinking, how the mischief it ever got up !"

There are several points from which the Falls can be seen —the suspension bridge from the American to the Canadian side, and Goat Island, on the United States side. Two shillings is the toll for going over the bridge, and the same sum is also charged for going on to the Island. I prefer the Goat Island view, as this enables the visitor to have a good sight of the

American Falls and to get quite near the Horseshoe Falls. In crossing the bridge on to the island there is an admirable view of the Cataracts, which forms a very fitting prelude to the Falls; tons of rushing water tumbling headlong over stones so large that years have not displaced them. Those cataracts alone are worth travelling miles to see. Passing through an avenue of trees on the island, the nearest of the Falls will be noticed by the deafening noise.

On descending a long staircase, the visitor will soon be alongside the American Falls, so termed because they are entirely on American soil; and then a short walk further, and the Horseshoe Falls are reached. When I visited the place, a single plank bridge led to a small platform, which overhangs a portion of the Falls. This platform was strangely insecure at that time. A single rail round it was all the protection there was against persons falling over; but long before reaching the Falls the tourist will have well learned that the great American people have to take care of themselves, and if they cannot do that the Government will not for them. Simply a hasty glance does not realise Niagara. It is requisite to stand there and drink in the scene gradually, and then the first feeling of disappointment disappears, and gives place to an indescribable sensation of awe at its grandeur. The precipice over which the water falls is estimated at 160ft. in depth, and the entire width is about 1800ft., the shape resembling a horseshoe, and hence the name. No less than 100,000,000 tons of water is believed to pass over the ledge every hour, that is nearly 1,500,000 tons every minute, or about 25,000 tons every second or beat of the pulse. The air has been full of plans and projects during the last few years for utilising the Falls in turning some gigantic water-wheel or electric motor, but up to the present moment, fortunately for lovers of nature, no step has been taken to do this. As I stood there watching that fierce rush of water, I felt my hands and face becoming covered with the spray, which, arising as it does from the great trough at the bottom, forms a sight of itself. The lunar bow and the solar bow are formed with this spray rising far above the edge of the precipice; the former visible when the moon is full and sufficiently high in the heavens; the latter always when the sun shines on the Falls, and it makes an exceedingly pretty scene.

There are few words I have read respecting Niagara which so thoroughly describe the feelings of many of those who visit this scene—a piece of handiwork from Nature's quarry, untouched by human hand with mallet or chisel — as the words of Charles Dickens: "Then, when I felt how near to my Creator I was standing, the first effect, and the enduring one—instant and lasting—of the tremendous spectacle, was peace. Peace of mind, tranquillity, calm recollections of the dead, great thoughts of eternal rest and happiness, nothing of gloom or terror. Niagara was at once stamped upon my heart, an image of beauty; to remain there, changeless and indelible, until its pulses cease to beat for ever."

The majority of visitors seeing Niagara for the first time would naturally wish to descend the staircase and go right under the Falls, and it is only by so doing that the force and volume of the cataract can be adequately realised. The small sum of 2s. is charged for an oilskin suit, and down a rough staircase the traveller descends. This staircase is enclosed in a wooden shaft, fixed with iron clamps to the rock. The air is stifling, both in the staircase and at the bottom, and the spray fills the eyes, the mouth, and the nostrils. A few only who go down penetrate beyond the lower part of the staircase, as to do so entails climbing over slimy boulders. To the sure of foot it is well worth while doing so, as the over-arching canopy of rock, with the incessant downpour of water, increases in the mind the idea of vastness. The dashing of the spray, the cold winds, and the slippery condition of every inch on which the foot may be placed, prevents a lengthened stay below.

The Niagara Falls.

The Suspension Bridge previously referred to is deserving of more than a passing notice. From tower to tower it is 800ft. long, and is 258ft. above the water. The cost of it is put down at £100,000, and it was finished in 1855. The carriage and foot way is immediately underneath the railway track, the depth between the bottom of this and the footway being 28ft.

Other points of interest in connection with the Falls may be mentioned:

Terrapin Tower, at the edge of the Canadian Fall, which gives an opportunity to look almost perpendicularly down the cataract.

Table Rock, higher up on the Canadian side, immediately at the verge and edge of the Horseshoe Fall. This is a favourite spot for visitors to stand.

The Sister Islands, three in number, connected by handsome bridges with Goat Island. From these a splendid view of the Upper Rapids can be obtained.

Burning Spring, a short distance above the Falls, on the Canada side, which are interesting as showing some singular phenomena of liquid combustion.

CHAPTER XIII.

BUFFALO, CLEVELAND, AND DETROIT.

AFTER leaving Niagara Falls, it will necessarily be a matter of choice with the tourist what points of interest he purposes visiting afterwards. Buffalo, however, is such a convenient distance from the Falls, being only twenty-three miles off, that it forms a very convenient place for spending a night before proceeding. This city presents during the day all the aspects of a busy and thriving town. It is the third in order of size in the State of New York, and is situated at the entrance of Buffalo Creek and head of Niagara River, at the east end of Lake Erie. It is the point of entrance to the Erie Canal from the Lake, and as it possesses a water-front of about six miles, it enjoys an immense grain and timber trade.

Six or seven different railways run into the station which connect it with all parts of the country, and this, with its canal and lake traffic, has made it one of the most important distributing cities in the States. Its population in 1880 was 155,134. Iron, tin, brass, and copper occupy a very important place in its industries, and malting and brewing are also largely carried on. The grain elevators will be a source of interest to most visitors, and an effort should be made to look over some of the large iron-works. A public park, embracing between 500 and 600 acres, and divided into three plots, is one of the chief points of interest. Spacious thoroughfares connect them and form a continuous drive of nearly ten miles. This park is very picturesquely laid out. A splendid International Bridge, crossing the Niagara River to the Canadian village of Fort Erie, was completed in 1873, at an enormous cost. The American end of it is at Black Rock, a suburb of Buffalo. Its chief streets are Main, Delaware, and Niagara, and these, with others, are bordered with a profusion of trees. Buffalo has, in fact, gone in for these trees largely, and their shady and pretty effect is best noticed in the squares named Niagara, Lafayette-place, Franklin, Washington, Delaware-place, and Terrace-parks.

Among the public and prominent buildings the following may be named: St. Paul's Cathedral (Episcopal), in Pearl-street; the State Arsenal, in Batavia-street; the State Armoury, in Virginia-street; the General Hospital, in High-street; Court House, and City Hall, Franklin-street; St. Joseph's (Roman Catholic) Cathedral, and the State Asylum for the Insane, which the Buffaloites claim to be largest in the States, if not in the world. Its frontage is about 2700ft., and the grounds attached to it cover some 283 acres. How many disappointed kings and queens and presidents there are in this admirable institution, I do not know.

The hotels are: the Mansion House, Tifft House, Main-street, and the Continental, near the Depôt, all of them at the usual rates.

Within very easy distance of Buffalo is Cleveland, where the late noble President of the States lies interred. It is a charming district, and has for this and other reasons had a very rapid growth. In 1830 the population was only 1000, now it is over 160,000. It is very fitly called the "Forest City," for its rich abundance of trees, especially maple and elm, makes it well deserving of this name. The main portion of the city stands on a gravelly plain, elevated some 100ft. above Lake Erie, on the south shore of which the city is situated. A river passes through it in a winding course, affording a capital harbour for the numerous coasting steamers and schooners, and which carry on a considerable trade with Canada. There are several handsome bridges across the Cuyahoga, the river referred to, which connect the different portions of the city.

Cleveland, with the other parts of the city, named Brooklyn and Ohio, contains between ninety and one hundred churches, and the little edifice where the late President Garfield was accustomed to worship, should be an object of interest, as also his tomb, which has been guarded up to the present by a small detachment of United States soldiers. Euclid Avenue is the fashionable part of the city, and is lined with elegant residences, surrounded by extensive grounds. Monumental Park, although only some ten acres in extent, is very prettily laid out. There is a fine statue in the park of Commodore Perry, the hero of the battle of Lake Erie, which cost about £1600. The chief public buildings are the Post Office, Custom House, City Hall, Case Hall, a building used for lectures, public meetings, &c. A medical college stands on the shore of the lake, and on University Heights there is a Homœopathic Hospital, with which is connected a college for the same practice of medicine. As an evidence of one practical way which our cousins have of doing things, I may mention that the Cleveland City Infirmary has attached to it a good farm, which is worked by the inmates of the institution.

Hotels: Weddell House, corner of Superior and Bank-streets; Kennard House, and the American House.

It is a very pleasant sail across Lake Erie from Cleveland to Detroit, which is situated on the banks of the Detroit River. This is the largest city in the State of Michigan, having in 1880 a population of 1,282,772. It presents evidences of considerable wealth and commercial enterprise. Extending, as it does, for some eight miles along the river, which joins Lake Erie, ample space is thus afforded for mills, timber-yards, grain elevators, warehouses, and dry-docks, and it has thus lent itself naturally to the rapid development which it has experienced.

The original site of the city was visited by the French as early as 1610. In 1796 the United States took possession of it, but in 1812 it fell during the war into the hands of the British, and was recaptured in 1813. The Freight Depôt of the Michigan Central Railroad occupies an immense area, and near it are the Custom House, with the Post Office, Opera House, which claims to be one of the largest and most elegant in the country, and the Board of Trade buildings. The chief streets are Jefferson Avenue, Woodward Avenue, which crosses the former at right angles, and divides the city into almost two equal parts; Grand River Avenue, Fort-street, Michigan Avenue, and Gratiot-street, at different angles with Woodward Avenue. One of the finest thoroughfares is West Fort-street, which is a very fashionable locality; Lafayette Avenue bears a similar character.

The Grand Circus is the leading park, and is semi-circular in form. A short distance from this is the Campus Martius, an open space, 600ft. long and 250ft. wide. This is crossed by Woodward and Michigan Avenues, and Monroe Avenue and Fort-street radiate from it. Facing this square is the City Hall, considered the handsomest structure in the whole city. As cost is always an item of general interest with regard to public buildings in the States, I may mention that in this instance it is put down as £120,000. In front of the City Hall, which is some 200ft. long and 180ft. high to the top of the tower, is a soldiers' monument, to commemorate the Michigan soldiers who fell in the Civil War.

Churches of every denomination are found in abundance, and I would here remark that, with regard to places of worship, the majority of the cities of both the States and Canada have shown a commendable zeal in erecting edifices noted equally for their substantial and striking character and the taste and finish of their interiors. Church architecture, in fact, forms a prominent source of interest to most people visiting the States. Public libraries and the buildings of the Young Men's Christian Associations, again, form very striking features of the public spirit which has been displayed by our Transatlantic cousins in this respect. There are over 20,000 volumes in the public library in Detroit, and the Young Men's Society has a library of some 12,000 volumes.

The Hotels are the Russell House, at 3dols. 50 cents (14s. 6d.) per day; the Biddle House and the Michigan Exchange, from 3dols. to 4dols.

Pleasant excursions may be made by steamers on Lake Erie from Detroit by those so disposed.

CHAPTER XIV.

CHICAGO.

THERE is no other town or city in the entire States which has been so much talked and written about as Chicago. Even San Francisco, with its Golden Gate and perplexing Chinese problem, and which is considered to be so wealthy that some of its millionaires (in dollars) are said to light their cigars with twenty-dollar bills, sinks into insignificance when compared with "wonderful Chicago." All will remember the large fire of 1871, which is supposed to have arisen from a cow kicking over a lamp in a stable, and which destroyed some 209,000,000 dollars' worth of property, including about 25,000 buildings, covering an area of from three to four square miles. On the ruins of these, one of the finest cities in the entire Union has been built. Marvellous accounts reached this country of the rapidity with which buildings were erected. Even before the fire had exhausted itself plans were made for new streets and stores, and, with all the vigour of modern American enterprise, the major part of the present vast city rose towering above the ruins, a monument to succeeding generations of western progress. Amusing reports were heard of the commercial announcements of some of the ruined tradesmen, who had to begin business over again. "Nothing left out of the fire but a five-dollar bill, wife and four children—never say die," was not an uncommon appeal to the public.

In 1830 the population of Chicago was put down as 80, in 1870 as 298,977, and now it is considerably over 500,000. Of the growth in the value of property, it is quite unnecessary for me to quote the numerous statistics which might be given, but suffice it to say that the rise in the value of land and property has scarcely been equalled even by some portions of the City of London. A citizen of Chicago is reported to have said to an English visitor: "Our city is the biggest thing on the planet; we've had the biggest fire; we lifted the city five feet out of the mud; we made a river run up hill—it wouldn't go where we wanted it, so we turned it end and end about; and it's the only city on earth every inch of which is covered three inches deep in mortgages." Another denizen of that vast city has also the credit of saying that "New York has the money, Boston the brains, but we start the big ideas and carry them out with eastern money."

The site of the city lends itself admirably to the rapid progress which it has experienced. Situated at the southern extremity of Lake Michigan, it is in direct water communication with the spacious territory reaching from the north-west portion of Lake Superior to the Atlantic. Surrounded, again, as it is, by a network of railways connecting it with all the leading cities of the States and Canada, it is in communication by land with every important part of the country. These facts account for its marvellous development, and to what extent it may grow during the coming years yet remains to be seen. New Chicago may well claim the title of Queen City, for its buildings, streets, and general aspect are of the most striking character. Its streets are all laid out at right angles—in fact, in no city of the Union is the right-angle principle with regard to its thoroughfares so conspicuous as it is in Chicago, and some of its streets run to a length of from three to ten miles. Chicago River flows through the city, and with its numerous slips affords a water frontage of over forty miles; in addition to the lake front, where a splendid outer harbour has been constructed, this river divides the city into three distinct parts, which are known as the north, south, and west divisions. These are connected by between thirty and forty bridges and several tunnels under the river-bed.

The industries of Chicago are as multifarious as is its population. It would be difficult at the moment to say what is not manufactured there. Its grain trade is simply immense—a phrase so very applicable to many things American. The shipments in 1879 amounted to 129,851,553 bushels. The elevators for receiving the grain and transferring it to the railway waggons, when it is brought in by ship, are the largest in the country. They are towers of corrugated zinc reaching a height of 80ft. or more, and unload with a capacity of 7000 bushels each. The miles of water troughs to be seen along the streets show the vastness of the live-stock trade. Thousands of cattle, hogs, and sheep are driven into the city, and leave it in the form of tinned meats, hams and bacon, &c. Over three million head of these animals are now driven into the city every year, and of these nearly 2,000,000 are hogs. Now and again a shipload of wooden hams find their way out of the city, for Chicago can do a few things of that kind. A smart Chicagoan (when, a year or two ago, so much was said of a disease prevalent among the hogs) exclaimed: "You Britishers may call our ladies the most overdressed of any in the world; you may say that New York is the worst lighted and paved of any large city in creation; you may call our political life a mixture of jobbery and cheat, and we don't care a continental; but you say anything against our hogs, and every particle of American honour feels itself insulted and disposed to smash anything which comes in its way!" Thus highly do they value this trade. In 1880, it is said, the Chicago packers could find room for 300,000 barrels of pork, 400,000 tierces of lard and hams, and 90,000,000lb. of meat, or 140,000 tons of stuff, the product of nearly 1,250,000 hogs. One house claims that it can slaughter and dress 20,000 animals in a day. Who does not long to be a "hog merchant" with these facts before him? The progress of the animal from pig to pork and hams is a very brief one. Fifteen or twenty minutes represents the space of time to go through the whole operation of being killed and suspended in the large ice houses to get cool so that they may be properly seasoned before being boxed; but the further methods of dealing with this large business are not matters for us to inquire into at present.

The lumber trade is another gigantic industry in Chicago, so vast, indeed, that I will refrain from quoting any statistics. Much of this finds its way to this country in the form of floorings, mouldings, doors, sashes, &c. Brass foundries, brick yards, reaping machine and sewing machine manufactories, abound in the city, as also do flour mills, tanneries, breweries, and cotton mills.

The leading hotels in Chicago are among the largest and most handsome buildings in the country. Palmer House is a vast pile, occupying an entire block in State-street, between Wabash-avenue and Monroe-street. Its tariff ranges from 3dols. 50 cents to 6dols. (14s. 6d. to 24s.) per day. The Grand Pacific Hotel is six stories high, and has a frontage of 750ft. Throughout it is most luxuriously furnished, as is also the Palmer House. The dining hall of the Pacific is 130ft. by 60ft., and the scene in the entrance hall, called the Grand Exchange, during the business parts of the day, is one not likely to be forgotten. The tariff here is 3dols. 50 cents to 7dols. per day. The Sherman House and Tremont House are less expensive, being 3dols. per day, and are very comfortable houses. Less expensive places still are the Central Hotel, in Market-street, near Madison-street, at 10s. per day, and the Massasoit House, opposite the Union Depôt, at 8s. per day. Tramcars traverse the streets in all directions, the fare for the entire distance being $2\frac{1}{2}$d.

Carriages have a reputed fare of 2s. per mile, but the English visitor would be fortunate if he succeeded in hiring one at this rate.

The public buildings are the Court House, Custom House Post Office, and Chamber of Commerce, which last is one of the finest and most complete buildings of its kind in the world. Commercial gentlemen visiting the city should obtain an introduction from a member to visit the chamber from 11 a.m. to 1 p.m. The City Hall is a magnificent building. The University of Chicago occupies a beautiful site overlooking Lake Michigan, at Cottage Grove. The main building is 136ft. by 172ft. There are also several theological seminaries worthy of notice. Mercy Hospital, corner of Calumet-avenue and Twenty-eighth-street, is a very handsome building, with capital interior arrangements. The chief parks are the Lincoln Park and the Union Park; the former is on the lake shore in the northern division, and contains about 230 acres, and has five miles of drives and walks. The latter is in the western division; some £20,000 has been spent in this park on lakes, drives, hills, zoological and landscape gardens, &c. The smaller parks are Douglas, Lake, and Jefferson.

The most important streets are the Michigan and Wabash Avenues, State-street, and Dearborn, Clark, La Salle, and Wells Streets running parallel with Lake Shore, and Jackson, Adams, Monroe, Madison, Washington, Randolph, and Lake Streets, crossing them at right angles, and extending across the city from the lake.

One very prominent source of interest is the system by which Chicago is supplied with water. The waterworks are situated on the Lake Shore in the north division, and in order to obtain the purest water possible, a shaft has been sunk under the works, and a tunnel has been built out from it for a distance of two miles. At the end of this tunnel a water tower 130ft. high has been built, up which the water is forced by four engines having a pumping capacity of 72,000,000 gallons per day. There are also forty artesian wells supplying the city with fresh water, in addition to what is obtained from the lake. A splendid view of Chicago Lake and surrounding country may be obtained from the top of the tower, which is reached by a spiral staircase. Permission to view the works can be readily obtained from the chief engineer.

CHAPTER XV.

CINCINNATI AND LOUISVILLE.

THERE are several places north of Chicago well worth visiting, notably Milwaukee, the commercial capital of Wisconsin, and, next to Chicago, the largest city in the North-West. This is quite a large and flourishing town, covering about nineteen miles square. It has an immense grain and flour trade. The distance from Chicago is eighty-five miles, and the journey occupies from two to three hours. All interested in the grain and flour trade going out to visit America should certainly go to Milwaukee. The granaries of the Milwaukee and St. Paul Railroad have a storage capacity of 1,500,000 bushels, and an adjoining flour mill is capable of producing 1000 barrels of flour daily.

By many, however, and especially those going out for a very brief visit, Milwaukee would be omitted, and the traveller would strike south, intending most likely to travel direct to Cincinnati. The "Queen City" is the name which has been given to this town on the Ohio River. On the opposite side of the Ohio to Cincinnati are the towns of Newport and Covington, in the State of Kentucky. Built, as the city chiefly is, on two terraces, one 60ft. and the other 112ft. above the river, it naturally possesses a splendid position and scenery, and hence the pretty name it has derived as mentioned above. It may reasonably claim to have its streets well planned and built. They are laid out with great regularity, and are broad and much better paved than many other cities in the Union, some being well shaded with leafy trees, giving a very picturesque aspect. The more aristocratic residences on the higher terrace are built of blue limestone. There is considerable wealth in the city, as iron, furniture, boot, shoe, pottery, and machinery manufactories abound. Pork packing is also very largely carried on, its trade in this commodity ranking in importance next to Chicago. Its population is now about 260,000, and the city dates back its origin to 1788. There was, however, in its early history, much difficulty with the Indians, who retarded the progress of the town.

The public buildings of prominence are the U.S. Government Buildings, embracing the Post Office and Customs House. The City Municipal Buildings occupy a whole square in Plum-street. The County Court House would put into the shade many of our severely plain edifices for a similar use in this country, having an entrance porch with six Corinthian columns. The Chamber of Commerce in Fourth-street has a public hall which affords standing room for 25,000 people, and the Masonic Temple and the Oddfellows' Hall show to what extent these orders are favoured in the city, both buildings having a very handsome appearance, with elaborately ornamented interiors. The building of the Public Free Library is a very prominent structure, in the Romanesque style, and affords shelving room for some 300,000 volumes. There are a number of halls, where meetings, lectures, and entertainments take place during the winter months. One of these, the Greenwood Hall, in the Mechanics' Institute, is spacious and very conveniently arranged.

The Tyler-Davison Fountain in Fifth-street is a very conspicuous feature of the city. It stands on a freestone esplanade 400ft. long, and 60ft. wide. The lower basin is 40ft. in diameter, and in the centre of this is the Saxon porphyry base supporting the bronze work, which is 12ft. square. At each corner there are infant figures in bronze in a variety of attitudes, and there are also bas-relief figures around the base which represent some of the different uses of water to mankind.

From the upper part of the bronze base extend four large basins, and from the centre rises a column with vines ascending and branching off at the top, in the form of palm-leaves. Around this column are groups of statuary; and on the summit of it stands a large female figure with arms outstretched, and over the fingers the water rains down in rather an artistic and pleasing way. The entire cost of the work is said to be £40,000, and it was executed in Munich.

The other places of interest are: Eden Park, situated on a hill in the eastern part of the city. The park contains about 216 acres, and from it a splendid view of the city and the valley of the Ohio can be obtained. Burnet Woods, Lincoln Park, and Washington Park, are the other public pleasure resorts of the city. Spring Grove Cemetery comprises over 600 acres and claims to be one of the most beautiful in the West. It is very picturesquely laid out, and contains many fine monuments. The entrance buildings are a prominent feature, and cost about £10,000.

The suspension bridge connecting Cincinnati with Covington on the Kentucky side is a very handsome structure. The entire length of the bridge is 2252ft., and from tower to tower 1057ft.; the height from the water is 100ft.

There are many beautiful drives in the suburbs of the city, and the accommodation for transit from place to place is good, but cab hire is very expensive, as in other places in the States.

The hotels are: Keppler's, 12s. per day; Merchant's Hotel, 10s.; and the Grand Hotel, 16s. per day.

The city of Louisville is located on the Ohio River and is the chief town of Kentucky. It is situated at the Falls of the Ohio. A canal $2\frac{1}{2}$ miles long has been made to obviate the obstruction to navigation caused by the Falls. The cutting of this canal proved a very costly undertaking, as most of it was through solid rock.

Louisville thrives upon whisky and tobacco chiefly, and these being very profitable trades, the wealth of many of the inhabitants is evinced by the large number of large and elaborate residences.

The City Hall is the most conspicuous building, and is somewhat peculiar in style, having a large square clock tower. The Industrial Exposition buildings outside the city are worth a visit, especially if there is an exhibition in progress at the time. The State Blind Asylum is one of the finest institutions in the West.

The city is surrounded with pretty villages, of which the chief are Portland, three miles below the Falls; Silver Creek, four miles on the Indiana side; Harrod's Creek, eight miles up the river; and Lexington, the road to which is especially attractive. Jeffersonville is a good-sized town on the Indiana side, and connected by ferry and bridge, which is 5219ft. long, divided into twenty-five spans supported on twenty-four pillars. New Albany is another town on the same side as Jeffersonville, with a population of 16,422. A Louisville writer says: "From the hills at the back of New Albany one may look down on the large extent of Louisville, half-hidden beneath the foliage which surrounds so many of its houses; can note the steamers slowly winding about the bends in the Ohio, or carefully working their way up to the broad walks; can see the trains crawling like serpents over the high suspension bridge, and the church spires and towers gleaming under the mellow sunlight."

CHAPTER XVI.

ST. LOUIS AND PITTSBURGH.

St. Louis is one of the most important cities of the West, as well as one of the largest, and boasts what not many cities in the States can, an existence of upwards of a century. In 1764, it is recorded, there was a population of 120, and a further account says that "In 1790 a St. Louis merchant was a man who, in the corner of his cabin, had a large chest which contained a few pounds of powder and shot, a few knives and hatchets, a little red paint, two or three rifles, some hunting shirts of buckskin, a few tin cups and iron pots, and perhaps a little tea, coffee, sugar, and spice." To-day the St. Louis merchant is a very different personage, with an immense store and a vast stock. The city lies on the west bank of the Mississippi River, some twenty miles below the entrance of the Missouri, about half-way between St. Paul, at the head of the navigable part of that river, and New Orleans, at the mouth of the Mississippi. The city is built a considerable distance above the surface of the water, and covers an area of over twenty square miles, with a population, in 1880, of 350,518.

The steel bridge across the Mississippi is one of the principal sights of the city; it cost £2,000,000, and has the reputation of being one of the finest bridges in the world. It consists of three spans resting on four piers built of granite and limestone. The centre span is 520ft., the others 500ft. each; and each of them is formed of four ribbed arches made of cast steel. The arches rise 60ft., which allows the passage of any steamboat at any height of the water. The bridge is built in two stories, of which the upper has two carriage ways, two horse-car tracks, and two footways, and the lower has a double railroad track.

The Water Works, near the bank of the river, contain two pumping engines, each having a capacity of 17,000,000 gallons per day. The engine house is always open for visitors.

The chief public buildings are: The Four Courts, a very handsome edifice, between Eleventh and Twelfth Streets; and the Court House, which cost about £240,000, and is built in the form of a Greek Cross, with a lofty iron dome in the centre. The new Custom House and Post Office, at the corner of Olive and Eighth Streets, is well deserving of a careful inspection. The Merchants' Exchange, in Third-street, of grey limestone, is also very fine. The galleries are free to all visitors when business is proceeding, and the sight is worth seeing. The main hall is a room 102ft. by 81ft.

St. Louis can boast of several spacious parks and pleasure grounds, the aggregate number of acres covered by these resorts being 2000. Lafayette Park is the most beautiful. There is, however, no drive in it, but it is very tastefully laid out. Forest Park is the largest, and contains no less than 1350 acres. Tower Grove Park contains some pretty lawns and shrubberies, and covers about 277 acres. Shaw's Garden, near the last-named, was presented to the city a few years ago. The flower gardens in this are quite a source of interest. Hyde Park, Washington Square, Northern Park, and Lindell Park are other public recreation grounds.

St. Louis is famous for the number of its charitable institutions, and I may incidentally remark here that asylums for various objects form a very conspicuous source of interest in all the leading cities of the States. The sick, the maimed, the blind, and the insane, have all been well cared for.

There are a number of libraries, art galleries, churches, and educational institutes, some of which will be of considerable interest to many.

The hotels are: The Laclede, at 12s. per day; Lindell House, from 8s. to 15s. per day, according to location; and the Southern Hotel, the largest in the city, and the most expensive.

The industries of St. Louis are numerous, of which flour is the chief, something like 2,000,000 barrels per year now being produced. Hog packing, iron works, and other commercial enterprises are carried on with considerable push. The rivalry between cities on the other side of the Atlantic is very characteristic of the people. Chicago sneers at St. Louis as being slow and behind the necessities of the (American) age. In retort, a pamphlet has been published by order of the St. Louis County Court, and in it the bold author says, "Chicago is a depôt for speculators in grain, and Cincinnati abounds in hogs: but this is the end of their glory. . . . . St. Louis is destined at no distant day to be the great vitalising heart of the world's civilization!"

I have visited many towns and cities in the States, but I do not remember one where mud and dirt abounded as in the "iron city," as it is fitly termed. One part of Pittsburgh is appropriately called Birmingham, on account of the large number of iron works, and there are also in the same district numerous glass works. Pittsburgh offers nothing of interest to sightseers pure and simple, and they will find it only lost time to go there, but others who are desirous of seeing fully how rapidly America has progressed in its industries will do well not to leave Pittsburgh unseen. It is the second city in Pennsylvania in importance and population, there being now (1883) about 160,000 people within its precincts, a large number of whom are connected with the iron trades. The Alleghany River, which divides the city, is spanned by seven bridges, and five bridges cross the Monongahela River.

There are no public buildings particularly worthy of mention. Pittsburgh is essentially a business city, and makes no pretences. However far removed the visitor may be from the glass and iron trade, he cannot fail to have his interest aroused in visiting some of the works, and I may say here that there is no difficulty in obtaining permission to go over them. The American Ironworks alone employ over 2500 hands, and cover seventeen acres.

The only hotels which I need mention, as the choice is anything but good, are the Monongahela House at 16s. a day, and the hotel of the Union Depôt at 14s.

The following verses, by Richard Realf, in a recent issue of a San Francisco paper, take off in a capital way what Pittsburgh is famous for:

HYMN OF PITTSBURGH.

My father was a mighty Vulcan ;
   I am smith of the land and sea ;
The cunning spirit of Tubal Cain
   Came with my marrow to me.
I think great thoughts, strong-winged with steel ;
   I coin vast iron acts,
And orb the impalpable dreams of seers
   Into comely, lyric facts.

I am Monarch of all the Forges,
   I have solved the riddle of fire,
The Amen of Nature to cry of Man
   Answers at my desire.
I search with the subtle soul of flame
   The heart of the rocky Earth,
And hot from my anvils the prophecies
   Of the miracle-years leap forth.

I am swart with the soots of my turnace,
  I drip with the sweats of toil;
My fingers throttle the savage wastes,
  I tear the curse from the soil.
I fling the bridges across the gulfs
  That hold us from the To-Be,
And build the roads for the bannered march
  Of crowned humanity.

CHAPTER XVII.

THE OIL REGIONS.

WHILE referring to the Pittsburgh district it will not be out of place to give some particulars of the modern industry which has done so much to promote labour and create wealth in the State of Pennsylvania. During my journey to the States, three years previously, my time was chiefly absorbed in Canada and several leading American cities, but during the last journey, among my visits to various manufacturing centres, certainly the most agreeable were my peregrinations among the oil-fields of Bradford and Oil City. The present gigantic trade in burning oils sprung from a very insignificant beginning. It originated and developed with the railway system, and has grown to dimensions which can only be fully realised by a visit to the territories rich in an earthy sap which aids now in lighting most of the civilised world.

Notwithstanding the extensive use of gas and the later adoption of the electric light, illuminating oils not only retain their hold, but are rapidly increasing in consumption. I could give many statistics in proof of this, but to the general reader these would be uninteresting. Suffice it to say that during 1881 no less than 552,356,275 gallons of oil were exported from the States, and the Bradford district contributed a very considerable portion of this.

Bradford is about four hundred miles from New York, and

long before the district itself is reached evidence of what it is noted for is seen in the oil tanks scattered about everywhere in close proximity to the railroad track. I have seen many American towns, but none that I remember as so thoroughly

BRADFORD, PENNSYLVANIA.

typical of how towns rapidly spring up in America as Bradford. The engraving gives a good idea of what the district is like. The railway runs right across one end of the main street, and the depôt is adjacent. The "city" may, in fact, be said to consist of one long street and a few little ones, with houses, erected of wood, scattered about, and so covering a tolerably wide area. I spent some considerable time with the mayor, who informed me that the population was between 15,000 and 20,000. Almost the whole of the houses and many shops are built of wood, and the street pavements are of the same material; in fact, timber is everywhere the prevailing element; but long before an English visitor has reached Bradford, he will have become accustomed to wooden erections on all hands. Small as the town is, it supports three daily papers, and also boasts an opera house. There is vast accumulated wealth in the town, and, where money-making is such a powerful element, and the district itself may only be temporarily prominent, it is not reasonable to expect much in the way of street cleansing and sanitary arrangements, and these are conspicuous by their absence. Oil tanks and derricks are to be seen on all sides, and the most casual observer could not fail to notice evidences that the entire city, directly or indirectly, obtains its living out of oil. Bradford claims to produce, on an average, from 60,000 to 70,000 barrels of crude oil per day, and there were, the mayor informed me, 30,000,000 barrels on the surface of the earth, stored in the tanks, at the time of my visit. These tanks, made of iron, are as close together as is indicated in the illustration on page 97, and range in capacity from 2000 or 3000 to 3500 barrels (a barrel is 42 gallons)! They are 93ft. in diameter and 30ft. high. Fires occasionally take place at them, caused either by lightning or overflowing. The greater majority of those lost by lightning have been station tanks, with pipes running over the roof; but there have been tanks burned where the only pipe connection was through the shell near the bottom, the spark evidently going from the end of the swing pipe.

The derricks, erected of wood, run to a height of about seventy to eighty feet, as will be judged from the engraving given on page 99.

The artesian borings usually run to an average depth of from

750ft. to 1750ft., and often the oil will flow some 40ft. above the top of the derrick. The system of drilling is the same throughout the district.

Oil City, another important centre of the oil industry, possesses

OIL TANKS AT BRADFORD.

a similar character to Bradford, except that there are more buildings of a permanent character in it. If the stranger passes through Oil City in the evening or at night, he would be considerably surprised to notice that the only light for the entire depôt comes from a long pipe overhanging one of the goods sheds. The other end of this pipe has been driven down into a natural gas well, and for lighting all that is necessary is to perforate the end of the pipe above the station, and it at once breaks out into a blaze that suffices to illuminate not only the depôt, but four or five surrounding streets. Several towns are, in fact, lighted in this way, certainly at an extremely cheap rate; although it appears to be a somewhat singular method when viewed by English eyes, accustomed in the large towns of our own country to see in use some of the newest improvements in gas burners, throwing out a brilliant and well-diffused light.

The millionaires (in dollars, please remember) who have netted their wealth out of oil are very numerous. Oil is struck in a new district, and immediately there is a rush to it, and land advances to an enormous price in a few days. Garfield, one of the very newest oil towns in Pennsylvania, has very recently exemplified this. This district has been in the unfortunate predicament of being without water, and the quantity required for human existence there has had to be brought from a spring some considerable distance from the town. It has thus cost half-a-crown a barrel, but oil in the same district is worth only 2s. 4d. per barrel, and the water vendors have declined, it is said, to give a barrel of water for a barrel of oil. "Barrels, yet not a drop to drink!" must have been the cry of the Garfieldites.

I may mention that there is very little refining in Bradford, Oil City, and Titusville, another important town in the oil regions. The crude oil is simply stored in the tanks at these places, and is pumped through pipe lines which are laid down all the way from Bradford to Philadelphia, New York, and other places (a distance, it will be remembered, of about 400 miles), and there refined. A very large portion of this trade is in the hands of a gigantic monopolising company, who own newspapers, a trade paper, and many other organisations, by which they are specially enabled to operate in a very powerful manner, to the

WOODEN DERRICKS AT BRADFORD (PA.).

detriment of other producers and the purchasers. Seventy-five per cent. of refined oil is obtained from the crude, and the remaining twenty-five is used for benzoline, wax, and in other manufactures. It really is not at all to be wondered at that so much wealth is widely distributed in the States, when the fact is taken into account how largely Nature has contributed towards it in such resources as those to which I have been referring.

CHAPTER XVIII.

RICHMOND AND BALTIMORE.

RICHMOND is 344 miles from New York, and occupies some fourteen hours in the journey. It is the largest city in Virginia, and the capital of that State, a position it has occupied since 1779. Several important meetings have taken place in this city, which have affected more or less the entire United States. It was the scene, in 1788, of a Convention to ratify the Federal Constitution, and in 1861 it became prominent as the capital of the Southern Confederacy. It was defended with great obstinacy, and was at last fired by General Lee. It is said that about 1000 buildings were destroyed. At the present time its population is about 80,000, and it has a large trade in tobacco and flour.

The statue of Washington is one of the first sights of the city. It consists of a bronze horse and rider, of colossal size, on a granite pedestal of large proportions. Six bronze figures surround it. This very fine statue stands near the gate of the Capitol-square. The State Capitol stands in the centre of a park, some eight acres in extent, on the summit of Shockhoe Hill, one of the principal eminences upon which Richmond is built. In the centre of the building is a square hall, surmounted by a dome, beneath which stands another statue of Washington, in marble. Washington statues, and streets named after the great general, are as numerous almost as the towns and cities of the Union, and the Americans are not to be blamed for thus perpetuating the memory of one of whom they have every cause to be proud. The city has been very picturesquely laid out, and the James River, on which it is situated, has a winding but pretty course, being full of small islands.

At the north-west corner of the Capitol-square is the City Hall, and at the opposite corner is the Governor's house. The Post Office, in Main-street, is a handsome structure. Richmond contains many places of worship, some of which are very striking specimens of architecture, particularly the Monumental Episcopal Church, at the corner of Broad and Thirteenth Streets. The site was formerly that of the Richmond Theatre, but in 1811, during the performance of a piece entitled "The Bleeding Nun," the theatre caught fire, and in the commotion which ensued about sixty-nine persons were crushed or burned to death. On the spot the church was erected to commemorate the event, the remains of the victims being interred beneath a mural tablet in the vestibule.

The Hollywood Cemetery, in the western part of the city, embraces a considerable area, and is very beautifully laid out. Trees, shrubs, and flowers are to be seen in abundance. The remains of President Monroe and General J. E. B. Stuart are buried here. The soldiers' section contains the graves of hundreds of the Confederate dead. As will be gathered from this very brief description of Richmond, the city is not prolific in sights, but will be interesting to visit. Entrance to one or other of the tobacco factories could be obtained, and a sight of one of the immense buildings devoted to this trade would be sure to add to the pleasure of seeing Richmond.

The hotels are the Exchange and Ballard House, at 12s. per day.

Baltimore is the most important town in Maryland, and had in 1880 a population of 332,313. It is very picturesquely situated on the Patapsco River, about fourteen miles from its entrance into Chesapeake Bay. A well-constructed harbour has enabled the city to develope a good coasting and foreign trade in the products of the district—tobacco, cotton, petroleum, bacon, cheese, lard, &c. Large quantities of copper ore are also refined in the neighbourhood of Canton, a short distance from the city. Some of these smelting works employ a considerable number of men. Canning oysters, fruits, and vegetables are also important industries, and most people, whether from a business point of view or simply as consumers, could not fail to be greatly interested in these trades. No difficulty need be experienced in obtaining the necessary permission to visit the various works. Baltimore has been designated a "monumental city," on account of its many statues and their artistic value. The Washington Monument, in Mount Vernon-place, is one of the finest of many of the great General in the States. It stands upon a terrace 100ft. above tide water, and has a base 50ft. square, and 20ft. high. This supports a massive column, 176ft. high, at the summit of which is the colossal statue, 16ft. high. A height of 312ft. is thus reached above the level of the river. The fee, 15 cents, for entrance to the tower is well worth paying, as there is a capital view of the city and its surroundings from the top. The cost is estimated at £40,000. The Battle Monument ranks next in importance, and was erected to the memory of those who fell when defending the city in 1814. It is a Roman column with emblematical sculptures. The Wildey Monument, on Broadway, near Baltimore-street, is in memory of Thomas Wildey, the founder of the order of Odd Fellows in the States.

The most important streets are Baltimore-street, which runs east and west the whole length of the city, and contains many handsome places of business, and Holliday, Calvert, Fayette, Lexington, Madison, Park, Saratoga, and others. The favourite drives are through Druid Hill Park, *viâ* Charles-street, to Lake Roland, a distance of six miles, leading through a well-paved and shaded thoroughfare.

Among the public buildings is the Exchange, in Gay-street, a handsome structure, with a frontage of 240ft. There are on the east and west sides six columns of fine Italian marble, and a dome surmounts the building. The City Hall has been completed only seven years, and is considered one of the finest municipal buildings in the country. White marble has entered largely into its erection, and it fills the entire square enclosed by Holliday, Fayette, and two other streets. The Post Office and Custom House are close by the Exchange. The Maryland Institute in Baltimore-street is used chiefly for industrial exhibitions, fairs, &c. The Peabody Institute, at the corner of Charles and Monument Streets, contains nearly 60,000 volumes, and is free to all. Other libraries are: Odd Fellows' Hall, about 30,000 volumes; Mercantile, about 32,000; Maryland Historical Society, over 10,000. Church architecture forms a prominent feature in Baltimore, the Catholic Cathedral being especially imposing. Almost every denomination is well represented.

Druid Hill Park, already named, is the principal park of the city. It covers 680 acres, and is situated in the northern suburbs; rural beauty is the chief feature of this park. At the head of the lake is a tower, from the top of which a capital view is obtained of the city and harbour.

The hotels are: The Eutaw House and Maltby House, at 12s. 6d. per day; Howard House, in Howard-street, near Baltimore-street, is a comfortable house, at 8s. per day.

CHAPTER XIX.

WASHINGTON.

WASHINGTON well deserves its name of "the City of Magnificent Distances." Mr. G. A. Sala said of this city, some years ago, "that it would be the most magnificent city on that side the Atlantic, and some of its edifices, as, for instance, the Post Office, the Patent Office, and the Treasury Buildings, are really magnificent in proportion and design, but it is not quite begun yet. It contains certainly some noble public buildings, but they are scattered far and wide, with all kinds of incongruous environments, producing upon the stranger a perplexed impression that the British Museum has migrated to the centre of an exhausted brickfield, where rubbish may be shot, or that St. Paul's Cathedral, washed quite white and stuck upon stone stilts, has been transferred to the centre of the Libyan Desert, and called a Capitol." Since the time this well-known journalist wrote these lines, many of the vacant spaces have been built upon with either private residences or places of business, but there is still plenty of breathing room in and around the city. Its site is an admirable one, and was selected through the agency of General Washington, who laid the corner stone of the Capitol on 18th Sept., 1793.

The population is put down at 150,000; this, however, is largely increased when Congress is in session, and the interest in the visit of the tourist would be greatly enhanced if he were in Washington at such a time. The Congressmen and Senators, being paid for their services, can afford to spend the business part of the day in the work of the country; and so in both Houses the sittings commence at noon and do not very often extend into the night, as they do at St. Stephen's. Members of Congress receive £1000 per annum, and senators £2500, and, in addition to this, they are allowed mileage expenses, according to the distance which they travel to and from their homes to Washington, in order to attend to their parliamentary duties. It can scarcely be wondered at, with this incentive, that politics should be so much in the hands of professional politicians who make a living thereby. There is no difficulty in strangers obtaining access to the galleries, and there are few of the "male persuasion," at least, on a visit to America who would not desire to spend as much time as possible in the precincts of Congress, in order to see for themselves something of the legislative proceedings of the country. The Capitol and other public buildings, I may here mention, are open to the public every day, Sundays excepted, from 10 a.m. to 3 p.m. There is no fixed fee for being shown over them, but I never yet discovered an official in such places who declined a gift for services of this nature.

The Capitol is what it claims to be, one of the largest and most elaborate buildings in the world. The hill upon which it is built is 90ft. high. The main structure is 352ft. long and 121ft. deep, and each of the two wings is 238ft. by 140ft. The entire length is 751ft., and the area covered is $3\frac{1}{2}$ acres. Pure white marble enters largely into the materials, and this is always beautifully clean, so that when the sun is shining the effect is dazzling. Handsome grounds surrounding are beautifully laid out with landscape gardens, trees, and plants, and groups of statuary are distributed, some of which well merit close inspection. The main front has an immense colonnade and portico, with statues of Columbus, Washington, and allegorical figures of

"Peace and War," "Civilisation," &c. The bronze door which forms the entrance to the Rotunda from the east portico was cast at Munich. It is 17ft. high and 9ft. wide, and weighs, it is stated, 20,000lb. It is divided into eight panels, each containing a scene in the life of Columbus, and between the panels are sixteen statuettes, representing some of the contemporaries of the discoverer.

The dome is, of course, a prominent feature of this immense pile. It rises to a height of 400ft., and is crowned with a colossal statue of Freedom. A spiral staircase leads up to it, and the view afforded of the surrounding country should not be missed. The fresco painting on the corridor near the staircase, covering some 6000ft. of space, is remarkable for good grouping and careful execution. In the Rotunda, immediately underneath the dome, are eight fine historical paintings executed specially for the Government. The subjects are "The Declaration of Independence," "The Surrender of General Burgoyne," "The Surrender of Lord Cornwallis," "General Washington Resigning his Commission," "The Landing of Columbus," "The Embarkation of the Pilgrim Fathers," and others, which cannot fail to occupy much of the attention of the visitor.

The Senate and the Representative Chamber, the former in the north wing and the latter in the south wing, are both large, and very elaborately finished. The Hall of Representatives is 139ft. long, 93ft. wide, and 36ft. high, and the Senate Chamber is 113ft. long, and about 80ft. wide. Both halls are very tastefully decorated. Costly staircases are the means of access.

The Library of Congress, now containing about 450,000 volumes, is in the western portion of the building. It is the law of the country that to secure copyright a copy of every work published in the States must be deposited there. This part of the Capitol is, in fact, the British Museum of America. The old Hall of Representatives is now used as a National Hall of Statuary. It is semi-circular in form, and contains twenty-four columns. The ceiling is painted in panels, and light is admitted through a cupola in the centre, as in the Pantheon at Rome. Statues of celebrated Americans fill the hall. The President's and Vice President's rooms, the Speaker's, Senators' Reception, and some of the committee rooms are lavishly furnished.

The White House is almost as well known, by name at least, on this side the Atlantic as Windsor Castle. It is a plain but very substantial structure, some portions of it dating back to 1792. The material is freestone, painted white; it is 170ft. long, and 86ft. deep, and is two stories high. The building has a colonnaded front, but otherwise has no particular architectural merit, and were it not for its importance as the official residence of the President, it would be passed by as not being specially worthy of notice. It is close by the River Potomac, and for some reason the Washington sanitary authorities do not consider that in the summer it is one of the healthiest residences in the city. The "East Room" is the grand parlour, and the Blue, Red, and Green Rooms are on the same floor. Luxuriousness and costliness are two very conspicuous elements in the decoration and furnishing of these rooms. The East Room, I may mention, is 80ft. long and 40ft. wide. The Executive Office and Cabinet Room are on the second floor. Access to the public rooms of the White House from 10 a.m. to 1 p.m., when the President and family are in residence, is easy. No court or evening dress is necessary, except at receptions.

It may be interesting to note here that white ties and dress coats in the evening are in vogue in all the leading cities of the Union. I have attended political meetings where they have been general, and at a church tea party there would scarcely be a gentleman present who was not thus attired; in theatres and other places of amusement they may be counted by the score, and even a "quiet evening" at a friend's house would scarcely be complete if this custom of civilisation were not observed.

Theoretically, Americans abhor the conventional, but in reality they bow down and worship not only titles but high-sounding gratuitous diplomas, with a persistency at once surprising and perplexing. Notwithstanding, they are a warm-hearted hospitable people, possessing many admirable traits of character.

The commotion at the Capitol and the White House during the congressional session is peculiarly American; representatives may be seen by the dozen simultaneously discussing in certain places politics and tobacco. Copies of the *Congressional Globe*, the official record of the speeches, should be obtained as mementoes of what could not fail to be to all a pleasing reminiscence of a visit to a noted city. Members may begin a speech, and if with an eye to re-election by their constituency they desire to make a long one, they may easily get the permission of the House to have the whole printed in the *Globe*, having actually only delivered the first portion, and the entire speech is thus accepted as having been made in the House. Read speeches are very common, the percentage in fact of representatives who speak extempore being small, and without claiming to be acquainted with every detail of American political life, I can only mention that on more than one occasion I heard it stated that writers for the newspaper press are in some cases the authors of read speeches.

The Treasury Department is not far from the White House, at the corner of Pennsylvania Avenue, and is open to visitors from 9 a.m. to 2 p.m. The east front is modelled after the temple of Minerva, at Athens, and is 342ft. long, with an unbroken front of Ionic colonnade. There are in all about 200 rooms in the building. The cash and the gold rooms are of extraordinary strength, and possess decorative combinations of considerable merit. In the latter room there is usually stored about £2,000,000 in coin. Strangers are often granted the privilege of inspecting the rooms by permit of the treasurer. The printing of paper money, carried on in the upper and lower portions of the structure, may also be seen, and is of considerable interest.

The State, War, and Navy Departments, built of granite, are a magnificent pile of buildings, entrance to the public rooms of which can be readily obtained. These buildings are among the newest public structures in Washington. The Navy Yard, situated about one-and-a-quarter miles south-east of the Capitol, covers some 27 acres. The Ordnance Foundry and shop for the manufacture of guns, shot, and shell, are opened to visitors, under the direction of a guide. The museum contains an interesting collection of fire-arms, warlike munitions, and relics. Guns and other old trophies are to be seen also scattered about the yard.

The Patent Office is a very interesting building to inspect; it is located on F street (many of the streets in Washington are designated by letters). The Model Room is open from 9 a.m. to 3 p.m. The contents of these large rooms, which were in considerable confusion some time ago, are as multitudinous as they are various. The printing press of Benjamin Franklin, and many of the personal effects of Washington, would be sure to attract the attention of the visitor. Mechanics and those possessing more or less ingenuity would spend a good portion of their stay in Washington at this Patent Office. Some of the models are marvels of skill and precision, and are connected with every industry which the New World has yet seen, from the making of a toasting fork to a locomotive.

The Washington Monument reminded me strongly of Scotland's Folly at Edinburgh—a grand conception uncompleted.

The Botanical Gardens, National Observatory, and the United States Arsenal are other objects of interest.

The Corcoran Art Gallery, at the corner of Pennsylvania Avenue and Seventeenth-street, is the gift of a banker, whose name it bears. It contains a good selection of pictures, porcelain, and other pottery ware. The Smithsonian Institution stands in inclosed grounds, covering over 52 acres. This noble institution was founded by an Englishman for the increase and diffusion of knowledge. It is 447ft. long by 150ft. wide, and has nine towers, ranging from 75ft. to 150ft. high. The Museum of Natural History and kindred collections is very extensive and worthy of close inspection. The Columbian and the Howard Universities, the Louise Home, and the Soldiers' Home should also be visited.

Georgetown, about two miles from the Capitol; Alexandria, seven miles from the city, on the banks of the Potomac River; and Mount Vernon, fifteen miles below Washington, are interesting places, the last particularly, as containing the tomb of Washington. This is a plain but solid structure, built of brick, with an iron gate, through the bars of which may be seen the marble sarcophagi containing the remains of George and Martha Washington.

The hotels are Ebbitt House at 12s. 6d. per day; the National, at 12s. 6d. and 14s. per day; and others. Boarding houses may be found in all parts of the city at 30s. to 80s. per week.

CHAPTER XX.

PHILADELPHIA.

I DO not know of any more interesting city in the entire Union to visit than this, the city of brotherly love, or Quaker city. Its founder, the celebrated William Penn, said of it, "Of all the places I have seen in the world, I remember not one better seated, so that it seems to me to have been appointed for a town, because of its coves, docks, springs, and lofty lands." What was the exact locality of these places in the days of this worthy member of the Society of Friends is a matter of some little wonder to the modern tourist; the city lies between two navigable rivers, the Delaware and the Schuylkill, six miles above their junction, and only ninety-six miles from the Atlantic. It is the second city in population to New York, and is more thoroughly American, both in its streets and people, than is the Empire city, with its cosmopolitan inhabitants. In 1880 the census returns showed the number to be 847,170 against 674,022 in 1870. Founded in 1682 by the little Quaker colony, the impress of the sturdy, vigorous, and conscientious nature of that sect is stamped indelibly on its citizens of to-day, and the city is associated with the most important events which have occurred in the history of the New World. Its charter was bestowed in 1701, and the city has since prospered rapidly. The first Congress assembled here, holding its sittings during the troublous times of the War, and on 4th July, 1776, the Declaration of Independence was signed in the old hall, to which I shall refer later. We in England have little conception what a great day this 4th of July always is all over the States; and really our cousins are very remarkable for the ecstatic joy that they universally give way to on this anniversary, which they usually extend beyond the day. A perfect **Niagara** of oratory is poured forth; there are reviews, processions, bonfires, and fireworks innumerable all over the country, and it is rare that the day is got over without some lives being lost. In crossing the first time to the States I spent the 4th of July on the Atlantic; and a Boston gentleman, who had visited England many times, said to me that the greatest blessing of that voyage to him was the fact of being on the ocean away from all the noise and turmoil of its celebration. This Signing of the Declaration of Independence is deservedly an epoch in history, and in American literature and in general intercourse many things date from it. An American schoolboy being asked some question about the Reformation, in reply shook his head, and said, "I guess it must have occurred before the signing of the Declaration of Independence."

One of the oldest guide books says that "the original plan of the city was a parallelogram two miles long, from the Delaware to the Schuylkill, by one mile wide, and contained nine streets, running from the Delaware to the Schuylkill, crossed by twenty-one running north and south. In the centre was a square of ten acres, and in each quarter of the city one of eight acres, for public promenades and athletic exercises. This plan, so far as the arrangement of the streets is concerned, is still substantially adhered to." It is now claimed for it, and it may appear almost incredible, but may, nevertheless, be accepted as being the case, that it has considerably over 1000 miles of streets and roads, the majority of which are well paved, and underneath which is an admirable drainage system. Its population are well housed, well educated, and it is the experience of myself and many with whom I have come in contact, that more ordinary courtesy and attention are met with in Philadelphia than in any other city in the Union. The policemen and railway servants, as a class, it will very soon be discovered, are not overflowing with politeness; in fact, I have known civil inquiries from both treated in New York and other places with a gruffness gross and repugnant. A large number of these officials on the other side of the Atlantic might with advantage go to school to their fellow officers in Philadelphia. The working classes are, as I have remarked, well cared for. Madison-square and other parts of the city have been built upon with houses specially suited to their requirements, and between the two rows of houses there is a pretty strip of garden and children's play ground. Every possible organisation exists for the benefit of every conceivable form of want that charitable sympathy can provide for. I was considerably amused to notice a large signboard showing the rooms of the "Association for Promotion of Marriage among Germans." Whether similar societies with this benevolent object in view exist for the benefit of emigrants of other nationalities settling in that district, I do not know.

Of the antiquities, if we can apply this term to erections of a little over a hundred years old, the Independence Hall would, no doubt, be one of the first sights visited. It is in Chesnut-street, between Fourth and Fifth-streets; it was commenced in 1729 and completed in 1735. In the east room of the main building the Declaration of Independence was signed in 1776. It was afterwards read from the steps of the building to the crowd, which had assembled in State House Yard. Liberty Bell, rung at the time of the Declaration, occupies an honourable position in the hall. On it is inscribed, "Proclaim liberty throughout the land to all the inhabitants thereof." The room is full of old relics, such as the furniture used by the Congress at that time, and portraits of the country's worthies. The entire Declaration, which could be repeated by every school-boy in America, is too long to quote in full, but, as it may, perhaps, not be familiar to some, I will give the closing paragraph of it, which is as follows: "We, therefore, the Representatives of the United States of America in General Congress assembled, appealing to the Supreme Judge of the world for the rectitude of our intentions, do in the name, and by the authority of the good people of these colonies, solemnly publish and declare: That these United Colonies are, and of right ought to be, Free and Independent States, they have full power to levy war, conclude peace, contract alliances, establish commerce, and to do all other acts and things which Independent States may of right do. And for the support of this Declaration, with a firm reliance on the protection of Divine Providence, we mutually pledge to each other our lives, our fortunes, and our sacred honour."

The simple grave of Benjamin Franklin, one of the chief signatories to this Declaration, is in the graveyard of Christ Church, near the Independence Hall. It can be easily seen through the railing from the street. This church was commenced in 1727, and is still in a good state of preservation. Its steeple is 196ft. high, and contains the oldest chime of bells in America.

Other objects of antiquarian interest are the old Swede's Cottage, in Swanson-street, built in 1700; Ponn's Cottage, a two-story house off Market-street; Carpenter's Hall, built in 1770, where assembled the first Congress of the United Colonies; Treaty Monument, a simple obelisk upon a granite pedestal, at the corner of Beach and Hanover-streets, marks the site where Penn made his memorable treaty with the Indians. The old elm tree under which it stood was blown down in 1810.

The general appearance of the chief business thoroughfares of Philadelphia is that of a busy, well-to-do character. Handsome business premises are to be seen on all hands, and the majority of these are very solid and durable structures. So numerous are these prominent commercial premises that a list of them would be rather long and to some, perhaps, uninteresting. A few, however, may be named. The *Public Ledger* Buildings, in Chesnut-street, is, I should say, the finest newspaper office in the world. It is five stories high, and is built of brown stone. Mr. Child, the proprietor of the *Ledger*, and also owner of the building, is one of the wealthiest men in the entire city, and, indeed, it might be said the States, which is saying much. He is at the same time one of the most generous of Philadelphia's many eminent citizens. Every Sunday he may be found opening the pews of the church where he regularly attends, so that he might be termed the richest pew-opener in the universe. He is unostentatious in manner, but possessing the well-merited character of strict probity and conscientiousness. Philadelphia owes much to him, and this is freely acknowledged.

Other buildings are the Commercial Exchange, Second-street, below Chesnut-street, standing by the side of the old slate-roof house of William Penn; the premises of Messrs. Lippincott and Co., publishers, which are large and of noble aspect; the Guarantee Trust and Safe Deposit Company; the Custom House and Post Office in Chesnut-street, between Fourth and Fifth-streets, built in imitation of the Parthenon at Athens, and for which it is claimed that it is one of the finest specimens of Doric architecture in the States. The old Masonic Temple is another building of prominence, and so also is the new temple of the brotherhood of the mystic tie at the corner of Broad and Filbert-streets. Dry goods' houses, fine-art depôts, jewellery establishments, and a thousand and one other stores would not fail to interest all. It might be that now and again incidental bits of humour would occur in some of these stores; as, for instance, a young lady attired in a sealskin sacque of considerable value, was heard to say, in one of the fine art galleries, "Oh! ma! do look at those terra firma ornaments at the other side of the room, a'int they just lovely?" There is also a story told of a lady parading magnificently and making purchases, in one of the Chesnut-street jewellery stores. Two ladies were watching her, and one whispered to the other, "Evidently shoddy!" The grand dame overheard her, and answered, "No, madam, petroleum!" The largest of these stores connected with various trades are situated along Chesnut, Arch, Walnut, Broad, and Market-streets, which are all very spacious thoroughfares.

The most prominent public and educational buildings, taking them in the streets in which they are situated, are in Chesnut-street, always very crowded in the business parts of the day. The bridge over the river in this street is a very substantial structure. The Guarantee Trust and Safe Deposit Company is a somewhat peculiar but handsome building, made of pressed bricks, ornamented with Ohio stone and coloured tiles. Security against fire and thieves are of course the chief features of the building. Between Fourth and Fifth-streets the Custom House buildings are situated, to which I have already referred. Opposite this is the Farmers' and Mechanics' Bank, a handsome structure in white marble. Close by the Custom House is the old Post Office, an imposing marble building. The new Post Office, however, at the corner of Ninth and Chesnut-streets, is a far more handsome erection, and cost about three-quarters of a million pounds sterling. The buildings of the American Sunday School Union are worthy of notice. On the north side of the street and crossing Thirteenth-street stands the United States' Mint. Ionic is the style of architecture, and the design was copied from a temple at Athens. The delicate and interesting operations of coining may be seen by visitors every day except Saturdays and Sundays. There are also other matters in the building which would arouse the attention of the visitor. The building of the Young Men's Christian Association is one of the finest structures of a similar nature to be found on the other side of the Atlantic. There are stores on the ground floor, but the majority of the upper floors are used for reading, class, and lecture rooms and libraries. Its imposing appearance and the immense outlay which on all hands is evident in it would at once suggest themselves to all seeing it for the first time. The membership of this institution is very large, and the rooms are daily visited by hundreds of young men. We have no Young Men's Christian Association buildings in Great Britain that will compare favourably with those in some of the leading cities of the more Northern States. Their work is of the most practical and beneficial character, and were the present the time I could give many facts to prove what a powerful lever of usefulness they are. At the junction of Thirty-Sixth-street, Darby-road, and Locust-street, stand the new buildings of the University of Philadelphia. The Science and Art Department of the College is one of the largest and most conveniently arranged of any college building in the country. It stands in a square covering over six acres; the frontage is about two hundred and sixty feet, and over one hundred in depth. The Medical Department is also a very handsome building, and adjoining this is the hospital, under the charge of the Medical Faculty of the College. There are private rooms for invalids who have means and wish to pay. The University building and grounds will be of considerable general interest to the tourist. This institution is one of the oldest in the country. It was an academy in 1749, a college in 1755, and promoted to the dignity of a university in 1779. It possesses a large library, and its professors are very able men. Visitors will have no difficulty in obtaining access to some portions of the college buildings. Walnut-street, a wide, well paved, and well lighted thoroughfare, contains the building of the Pennsylvania Railroad Company, and the Philadelphia and Reading Company. The offices of a number of insurance companies are here, and also several conspicuous for good architecture. This street has been much built upon during the last few years, and contains many large and important buildings.

Another important locality is Broad-street, which has its terminus at League Island, a low tract of land at the junction of the two rivers—the Delaware and the Schuylkill. This island has been used since 1875 as a naval depôt, and a visit to it should not be omitted. It is admirably adapted for the purpose. Churches and other places of worship are very numerous in this street, not a few of which are very handsome erections. Near to Pine-street is the Deaf and Dumb Asylum. Horticultural Hall is, as its name indicates, the home of floral beauty. This was the first institution of its kind in the country, being established in 1827. At certain seasons of the year the displays in this building are of a very magnificent character. The American Academy of Music is close beside the hall just referred to. This opera house may reasonably claim not only to be a striking and capacious building, but to have excellent seeing and hearing properties. The Academy of Music, the Alhambra Palace, and other places of amusement are also in this immediate neighbourhood. The Union League Buildings is a club house with a large patronage. The Public Buildings, including the law courts and offices of the Corporation, is among the finest of its kind in the States, and I am not aware of any public building in this country, not excepting even the Manchester New Town Hall, which can be compared to it. Its length is 486ft. north and south, and the central tower rises to a height of 450ft. The entire space covered is between four and five acres, and there are over 500 rooms. An immense sum of money, up to the present, has been spent on this building, and it is indicative of the public spirit which the Philadelphians have always shown. The School of Design for Women is also in this same street, and has proved itself a very useful institution. The new Masonic Temple, already referred to, in which there are nine lodge rooms, is very elegant. Its style of architecture is somewhat peculiar, a tower rising at one corner to a height of 230ft. The extensive use of white marble in the buildings of Philadelphia will strike most visitors; scores of doorsteps to private houses may be noticed of this material, and, this being the case, it will be readily understood how largely it enters into more important uses. This gives a beautifully clean appearance to most of the edifices; in fact, I do not remember in all my peregrinations over not a small area to have noticed this quality so conspicuously marked about buildings and thoroughfares as in the leading streets of the Quaker City. The New Academy of Fine Arts is another building well worthy of an inspection of both interior and exterior. There are also a number of streets branching off Broad-street, which are most picturesquely laid out; private residences abound in them, exhibiting all the wealth and taste to which I have previously referred.

I may mention, among other places of interest, the Girard College, on Ridge Avenue, founded by the late Stephen Girard, who died in 1831. The original bequest was £400,000, for the erection of suitable buildings "for the gratuitous instruction and support of destitute orphans." The site embraces some 42 acres, and from the main buildings there is a fine view to be obtained. The College is built in Corinthian style in marble, and is about 218ft. long, 160ft. wide, and 97ft. high. Blockley Almshouse, in Thirty-fourth street, the Blind Asylum, corner of Twentieth and Race-streets, and other charitable institutions which abound in the city are worthy of being visited, the necessary permission not being difficult to obtain.

The Centennial Buildings in Fairmount Park are still standing, but they may almost be described as a gigantic cage with but few birds in. It was intended to have a kind of permanent exhibition of American manufactures in them, but many had withdrawn their exhibits when I was last there. They have, however, much that would interest any visitor. The structure itself is of the most marked character, but seeing that the purpose for which it was erected is a thing of the past, it is scarcely necessary for me to give details of the size of its exterior or the dimensions of the Machinery, Memorial, Horticultural, and Agricultural Halls. When it was completed, and the exhibition in full operation, it was probably the largest building in the universe. Some parts of the park are very prettily laid out. Lippincott's Guide says that the park itself "arose from the necessity for a supply of pure water, the deterioration of which threatened to become not only an evil but a grievous calamity. The mills and manufactories on the banks of the Schuylkill were multiplying rapidly, and there was great danger that in the course of a very few years the river banks for miles above the city would be lined with factories and workshops, to the utter ruin of the stream on which the citizens depended for their supply of pure water. Just in time to prevent this catastrophe Fairmount Park was conceived." Over five miles of the river and six of an important tributary have been enclosed and preserved for ever from the pollution of manufacturing processes. Nearly 3000 acres are embraced in these public pleasure and recreation grounds, and every year adds beauty to them. There is boating in abundance; lovely glens and spacious drives, where the *élite* of Philadelphia take their airing. Ornamental gardening and a rich variety of trees and plants have added to the natural beauty of the grounds. The buildings of the Zoological Society are in the park. The aviary here is a very pretty and suitable building for the purpose. The buildings for the carnivora, the monkey and elephant houses, the bear-pits, &c., I must dismiss by saying that they are all fully tenanted, and the tenants more than earn their board and lodging by ministering to the amusement of the many visitors who go to see them. Sweet Briar Ravine, in the park, is a charming spot. It is not often that country seats are in a public park, but there are several in Fairmount Park, the chief of which is Belmont Mansion. Washington and Franklin often visited here; Talleyrand and Louis Philippe were also guests at the mansion. The building is now a huge restaurant. "Tom Moore's Cottage" is close by the house, on the river bank. The Wissahickon is a pretty stream winding through a narrow valley between steep and lofty hills, well wooded. There is much up this stream, such as the Creek, the Hermit's Pool, Hemlock Glen, and Glen Fern, worth spending much time amongst. The entire grounds of this vast park are most interesting, and the public spirit which prompted the acquisition reflects great credit on those—and the number is large—who have been mainly instrumental in the matter.

Some other objects of interest are the Philadelphia Library, sometimes called Franklin Library, founded by him in 1731. A marble statue of Franklin, executed in Italy, stands over the front entrance. The library contains over 100,000 volumes. Admission is free from 10 o'clock to sunset. The "Ridgway Branch" of the Philadelphia Library is a very fine building, with a frontage of 220ft., and a depth of 105ft. It contains a very large number of books. The Mercantile Library in Tenth-street, above Chesnut-street, contains about 120,000 volumes. The Athenæum, an imposing building, in Sixth-street, has in it some 20,000 volumes.

There are many large squares, some of which are beautifully laid out. Among these, Logan-square, covering seven acres; Independence-square, near Independence Hall; and Washington-square, diagonally opposite Independence-square, surrounded by a handsome iron railing. The chief feature of the latter square is that it contains nearly every species of tree that will grow in the American climate, whether indigenous or not. An interesting map of the square may be bought, showing the position of each tree. Franklin-square, at Sixth and Race-streets, is a very pretty promenade; Rittenhouse-square, at Eighteenth and Walnut-streets, is in a very aristocratic part of the city, and contains many elegant private residences.

The hotels are: The Girard House, Chesnut-street, the Colonnade, and the American, in the same street, at 12s. 6d. per day; the Central, in Arch-street, and the Ridgway, at the foot of Market-street, at 8s. per day.

CHAPTER XXI.

RAILROAD SCENERY OF PENNSYLVANIA.

PENNSYLVANIA is particularly noted for its pretty railroad scenery—in fact, as much, if not more so, than any other State in the Union. It is a proud boast of the Pennsylvanians that they had the second railway which was opened in America, for they have one dating back to 1827. At the present time the State has a network of railways, and several of them are the best constructed of any in the entire States, a feature which is of no inconsiderable importance in the estimation of all who have passed over the somewhat flimsy trestle bridges and badly constructed tracks of some other lines which could be mentioned. All making a tour in the States, whether simply on pleasure bent or with a view to settling down in the New World, could not fail to be interested in the scenery which would be observed in travelling by railway in almost any part of the State to which we are now more particularly referring. In many other parts of America the eye misses the pretty hedges which divide the fields in England, and as a substitute a rough kind of railing stands by the railway on both sides. All along, those which are immediately near the track are covered with advertisements of somebody's liver pills, or some marvellous oil never known to fail in curing anything and everything. Literally, if these advertisements, whitewashed on the railings, were placed together in a line they could not fail to stretch for hundreds of miles. Truly, the Americans are an advertising people, as everybody will soon find out who goes over there. Notwithstanding, however, that some charming spots are desecrated with quack advertisements, these will be overlooked in the presence of scenery, rich in hill, vale, water, and foliage, in the oldest State of the Union—Pennsylvania—forming the perfection of beauty.

The North Pennsylvania Railroad travels through Montgomery and Bucks divisions of the State, noted for their fertility, and trains loaded with grain and produce will be seen at certain times of the year conveying such freight to Philadelphia. The Lehigh Valley and Wyoming Branch joins this railway, well known as one of the chief anthracite coal districts of the States. Bethlehem, along this line, is an old-fashioned, but very pretty little town, only a short distance from Philadelphia. Its Moravian founders have left their mark upon it, as also upon Nazareth, ten miles north, another very picturesque spot, as is evidenced by many families from New York and Philadelphia going there to spend the summer months. The Lehigh River in this district winds in and out among the hills in a way that cannot fail to strike the visitor. The Lehigh Gap is the name of a narrow pass where the mountains close in the river; and railway, canal and river all struggle together for elbow room. Mauch Chunk is a favourite district near here, giving its name to a village closed in on all sides by lofty mountains. The town, as the Chunkites designate it, is right at the bottom of a deep ravine, where the sun in winter can scarcely find its way down. But in face of this drawback, hotels and pretty residences have been built, and quite a flourishing business is being done. The district will well repay a visit if the tourist has time to make it. There are some very heavy gradients along the line here, one rising to a height of 664ft., up and down which the train is moved by a stationary engine.

Romantic scenery abounds all over the Lehigh Mountains. Waterfalls and gorges are to be found in the out-of-the-way places, among which may be mentioned the neighbourhood of Mauch Chunk, the Chameleon Falls, Onoko Falls, Terrace Falls, Cloud Point, and Stony Creek. After leaving these places, the traveller may travel on into the Wyoming Valley, revealing a perfect panorama of beauty.

The Philadelphia and Reading railroad, about which we have, unfortunately, heard so much for some time past, runs through a very beautiful district over the greater part of its route. There are several depôts of this railroad in Philadelphia. The "Long road," as it is termed to distinguish it from the shorter branches, has its terminus in Thirteenth-street. It passes, first of all, on leaving Philadelphia, through the entire length of Fairmount Park, where the Centennial Exhibition buildings still stand, and of which I shall have something to say later. The falls of the river Schuylkill, over which the railway crosses, are an early sight after leaving the Quaker City. Valley Forge, along which the track runs, was, during the Civil War, the scene of much fighting.

Soon after leaving this district a long succession of peculiarly named places will be passed, such as Pottstown, Mingo, Aramingo, Monocacy, and Birdsborough. Reading, the county seat of Berks, will afterwards be reached, where the company's works for rolling stock are situated, and to and from which railways radiate to all parts of the States. Port Clinton, after leaving Reading, is a very romantic district, high and rugged hills causing sharp curves and stiff gradients of the railway. Pottsville, the "Mountain City," as it is termed, well deserves its designation, and a few miles below this place are Schuylkill Haven and Cressona, two small towns. Minersville, named from its being the centre of the coal regions, is not the bleak uninteresting spot that some of our English colliery districts are. Ultima Thule may be reached from the last-named place, and it is the end of that particular branch of railway.

The visitor will observe that he is now in one of the

wildest parts of the States, and, with all the ingenuity of American railway constructors, they have been unable to make a line across a tremendous ravine below Ultima Thule. Taking the other line of rails beyond the one just travelled, the route passes through Frackville. The railway here is constructed along the side of the mountain, and the Mahoney Valley will be particularly noted. Here mining operations are briskly carried on, and engineering skill, which has made a perfect network of narrow tracks for coal waggons, has been exercised to a surprising extent. There would be a choice of several routes from this part. If the tourist pass through Losberry Junction, he will see between that place and Catawissa feats of engineering skill with which we have little in this country to compare. The journey could be pursued hence through New Jersey to New York, or back to Philadelphia.

The Pennsylvania Railroad, opened in 1834, covers a large mileage, and runs through most picturesque districts. Its main route is to Pittsburgh. Bryn Mawr is a growing town, some nine miles from Philadelphia. Hence on to Susquehanna the route is very beautiful. Harrisburgh and Gettysburgh will afterwards be reached; near to the former town is the "five mile bridge," which, however, does not indicate the length of the bridge, but its distance from Harrisburgh. The bridge itself is a very handsome structure, about three-quarters of a mile in length. Further on is Lewiston, about thirty miles from the railway and well among the Alleghanies, affording mountain scenery of great grandeur. Look out for Altoona hereabout, and you will soon see the Horseshoe Curve, a sight not likely to be forgotten, and the name of which admirably explains itself. This is a difficult pass round the head of a narrow valley, where the road has been squeezed into a hollow of the hills till it takes the shape of a perfect horseshoe, and approaching trains on either arm run parallel, though but a stone's throw apart, until at the apex they meet and pass. Not far from this curve is Cresson, a town on the very summit of the mountain, 3000ft. above the sea. Johnstown and other manufacturing centres will be passed as Pittsburgh is neared.

There are numerous other railways in Pennsylvania, but I have, I think, said sufficient to indicate that there are many vast sources of interest in the State.

CHAPTER XXII.

MANUFACTURING CENTRES—TRENTON.

AFTER leaving Philadelphia, it will, perhaps, be convenient for most tourists, especially those out only on a brief visit, to turn their faces towards New York, by taking the Pennsylvania railroad; it passes through several important manufacturing districts, which cannot fail to be interesting to many. Trenton, the chief seat of the American pottery industry, is only fifty-eight miles from Philadelphia, and is very pleasantly situated at the head of navigation on the Delaware. Historically its chief interest lies in Washington having won his famous victory over the Hessians there on 26th Dec., 1776. It is a pretty little town of some 27,550 inhabitants. It is admirably adapted for its trade, having capital water and rail communication with New York and Philadelphia. According to the latest statistics, which, I may say, were corroborated by my own inquiries in April last, the present extent of the trade may be accepted as follows: Number of establishments, 29; capital invested, £380,500; greatest number of hands employed at any time during the year 1881, 2966; males above sixteen years, 1792; females above fifteen years, 441; children and youths, 644; average day's wages of skilled potters, 2·50 dols., or 10s.; average for ordinary labour, 1·25 dols., or 5s.; total amount paid in wages during 1881, £180,635; materials, £190,048; products during 1881, £468,267.

It will be seen from what has been said that this is not by any means an extensive industry in the United States. There are a few more potteries in Cincinnati and East Liverpool, Ohio, but several of these make only a common kind of brown ware. Trenton is the chief seat of the trade, and as the tariff stands as follows—earthenware, plain and printed, 40 per cent.; white china, 45 per cent.; and decorated china, 50 per cent.—it is greatly surprising that, with such a powerful nursing as this, the pottery trade has not developed much more rapidly than is at present the case. When compared to the Staffordshire Potteries, with some 150 manufactories, producing every description of ware, from the commonest earthenware dinner plate to the richest works of ceramic art, it must be confessed that Trenton rather sinks into insignificance. The number of kilns owned is the best criterion of extent of manufacture in the pottery trade. Two firms have ten kilns, and the fifteen largest manufactories in the district have a total of eighty-three. Of these, about ten are making less or more printed ware—that is, a ware decorated in one or more colours; but I was informed that about three only were doing underglaze printing, and the number decorating on the premises is also very small. By far the bulk of American ware produced is a heavy hotel ware, for which there is an immense demand. This is white, without the least decoration, and visitors to the States would scarcely fail to notice that every or nearly every hotel of importance uses this description of earthenware. It is very thick, and not a few have been impelled to make strong complaint against the eternal display of white tea cups, and plates of an *unpalatable* thickness. Mr. Oscar Wilde, who claims to be the high priest of Æstheticism, in one of the many lectures which he has recently been delivering in America, said to an aristocratic audience, in one of the largest New York theatres: "When I was in San Francisco, I used to visit the Chinese quarters frequently; there I used to watch a great hulking Chinese workman at his task of digging, and used to see him every day drink his tea from a little cup as delicate in texture as the petal of the flower, whereas in all the grand hotels of the land, where thousands of dollars have been lavished on great gilt mirrors and gaudy columns, I have been given my coffee or my chocolate in cups an inch-and-a-quarter thick. I think I have deserved something better." No doubt, Mr. Wilde did deserve something better. There can be no question, however, that a cultured taste is very rapidly progressing in America, which is creating an increased demand for better-class china, and decoration on English and French ware is now carried on very successfully and profitably by several firms in Trenton and East Liverpool. Female decorators are chiefly employed, and ladies with taste and skill in this way are meeting with very remunerative results from their labours. There is a strong disinclination among some English china and porcelain manufacturers to employ lady amateurs, and there is thus a great difficulty in the way of many ladies whose services in some firms could not fail to be an acquisition. There is no such disinclination in America, but, on the contrary, such labour is in good demand for both under and overglaze painting.

Being well acquainted with the condition of the English pottery trade, I was, I must confess, somewhat disappointed with the yet youthful condition of the American manufacturers, but doubtless the next few years will see a marked change, and I anticipate a rapid progress, both in the number of producers and in the class of wares made. I may say, with regard to the work of amateurs, as in London and elsewhere, several kilns have been erected in New York and other cities for the firing of china, and some ladies, I was informed, made quite a successful business in buying white ware, decorating it, having it fired at not a high rate, and then selling it to the fancy warehouses and dealers.

We last year sent from this country no less a value than £867,054 worth of china and earthenware to the United States, notwithstanding the heavy duties that I have already named. There is at present a great outcry among the Trenton manufacturers for more Protection. The Hon. Hart Brewer is a master potter, and represents Trenton in Congress. He is a most vigorous advocate for a higher tariff, and has exercised a personal influence in urging the Government to harass china and earthenware importers, which is one indication among many how politics with our cousins are made subservient to personal interests. The seat of sensitiveness is the trousers pocket, and if the general English commercial public could hear what frantic shrieks some of the American manufacturers are making for increased duties, they would be amused at the arguments, and as Englishmen would feel flattered at the compliment thus paid to our manufacturing capabilities. As I desire to cover as much ground as possible in this work, I will quote a few extracts from a speech made in Congress by Mr. Brewer, for these will serve to show the style of protectionist arguments, as well as Mr. Brewer's views of the necessities of the industry with which he is immediately associated. He said, in a long speech, on the 8th April, 1882:

"Mr. Chairman,—The question of Protection has been discussed from the origin of the Government, and will continue to be discussed until the great battle between enslaved and pauperised labour products and free and well-fed labour products is decided. I shall make no apology for debating a question which addresses itself to every State and every interest upon which our internal and external commerce depends. I am a manufacturer; I comprehend my own position, and the position of the labour I employ, and the exact effect a fair protection has produced on prices; I believe I comprehend something of the vast interests at stake in the United States. I shall therefore ask the attention of the House to such views as I may present in favour of that kind of tariff I believe essential to a full and fair development of our resources and to a full and fair protection of American labour.

"The tariff, as I shall proceed to demonstrate, is to determine the condition labour is to occupy. It is to determine whether one-half of our population is to be consigned to the condition of the labourer of England, or whether, in the manhood of liberties, and the grandeur of our resources, we shall make it the handmaid of capital, and, through the unity, go on achieving and developing until, independent in our own resources, we are able to show to the effete aristocracies of Europe the manhood of labour, the grandeur of its opportunities, and the glories of its triumphs.

"Take away the tariff, break down all barriers to open markets, let the English, Belgian, French, and German manufacturers flood our cities, our towns and our country with their products, produced at starvation wages, and sold at starvation prices, and what will be the result? Our manufacturers cannot manufacture because they cannot sell; they cannot sell because the value of their product is chiefly made up of labour, and American labour is double in cost for production to European labour. Free trade, then, either excludes the American product from sale, or it forces the American labourer to labour for and live on starvation wages. The American people will never consent to so wholesale a degradation. It would be to roll back the wheels of civilisation; it would be to revive all the servitudes of the past; it would be to consign millions of our artisans, our producers, our mechanics, to a hopeless future.

"It always has been the policy of England to keep us dependent upon her for everything we manufacture. She would enslave us to-day if she could. She spares no one. She killed the woollen factories of Ireland to protect her own. She annihilated every industry in Scotland which interfered with her own monopoly. She hampered and restricted the production of every article, while we were her colonists, which in the remotest degree interfered with her production.

"England would rule the industrial world. It is too late for her to think of ruling the United States. In every period of her domination she has excluded everything from her market she could produce unless it paid tribute to her treasury, or aided her to become mistress of the seas and ruler of the markets of the world. 'But,' say her free-trade propagandists, 'her markets are open, free trade is her policy, and perfect freedom of exchange is now the principle of her commercial code.' It is but the old politeness of the spider to the fly. By prohibitory tariffs she perfected her machinery, built up cities, created factories, and accumulated capital. By war she subjugated nations and made them her customers; India, and made her her slave; the South Sea Islands, and forced them to buy her products. By her navy she forced her merchantmen into every sea and her merchandise into every port, until she had gained a force, a perfection and an accumulation of means for manufacturing no people could equal, and to a point where she could defy competition.

"To reach this point she had subjugated labour to poverty, and poverty to hunger, until her factory operatives were mere slaves to bread, and beggars for wages, working for half the pay of the free, well fed, unfettered and working men of the United States.

"The condition of labour in England and generally in Europe, as compared with labour in the United States, is one of the forcible and unanswerable arguments why we should protect our country and our people from the degradation, poverty, and crime which low wages impose. To produce articles which depend for their value on the labour required to produce them, in competition with English or European labour, one or two facts must exist. We must bring the price of wages to the standard of European enslavement, or we must protect our manufacturers and our people by such tariff duties as will enable us to meet the foreign manufacturer in our markets.

" What, then, is the condition of the English labourer ? 'He lives in wretched tenements, in most cases unfit for human habitation.' 'He is generally confined to one or two rooms for a family, where comfort, cleanliness, and even decency is impossible.' 'They are ill-ventilated, dreary, dirty rooms.'

"Labour and capital are essential unities. They have to unite, join hands, and make but one interest, for their unity is essential to all manufacturing, to all production, and to all progress. A tariff is a bond of union ; it is safety to the one, it is security to the other. As the two elements are combined by its effects, so are wealth and comfort diffused. The best interests of society are promoted in the exact ratio that wages are increased. The tastes for comfort, elegancies, and enjoyments which educated life demand, should everywhere be attainable and everywhere be diffused. There can be no general prosperity, no real progress, where they are not interwoven with and made a part of civilised life. Low wages exclude them ; a tariff produces them. There is no stimulus to effort, no spur to energy, no promise to hope, so direct as remunerative wages. They lead to independence, which is manhood's highest purpose.

"Crime, ignorance, and destitution are the unfailing accompaniments of low or starving wages. It is inadequate wages which has made the operatives of England what they are. Good wages procure homes, improvement, education, self-respect ; low wages force men into hovels, degradation, and want. The American labourer, by virtue of the tariff, has had remunerative wages ; his position in society has shown the result. English labour, forced into low wages, forced into ignorance, and forced into want, has made the English labourer a mere drudge, a slave to subsistence, conscript to degradation. High wages cannot exist without a tariff. Free trade is low wages, it is servitude, it is ignorance.

" Labour is the source of all wealth. Manufacturing is the application of labour to raw materials to perfect them for use.

A tariff enables us to manufacture. Production is but another name for development. A tariff enables us to produce. Low wages are poverty, want, and suffering ; high wages are prosperity, plenty, and comfort. A tariff is the sole barrier between cheap labour and low wages and well paid labour and remunerative wages. In England, Germany, France, Italy, and Spain the labourer is a slave to subsistence; his life is one long struggle for bread. In the United States labour reaches beyond subsistence. It aspires to manhood, which cannot exist without comfort ; to respectability, which society denies to hunger, to want, and to dependence; to education, which cannot be procured without the means to secure it; to cheerfulness, and progress, and elevation, which the labourer cannot secure unless he can earn enough to save. A tariff helps the labourer to attain to manhood, to respectability, to comfort, to the surplus essential to elevation, to cheerfulness, and to saving.

"Why, then, diminish the tariff? To diminish rather than increase our manufacturing interests, when the whole people demand the policy of expansion, which is protection—when our common welfare demands the extension of our commerce which nothing but protection can insure? Agriculture demands a protective tariff, for agriculture can only be up to the fair measure of its prosperity when every order of industry is full of manufacturing, when every spindle is moving, when every forge is in blast, when every engine is moving, when the ring of the hammer, the sound of the shuttle, and the buzz of machinery tell the farmer that they who consume are at work. It is protection to labour from competition with pauperised and debased labour. It is protection to capital from the brigandage of English piratical manufacturing wealth, which, having accumulated power by centuries of oppression and profit in dominating over the markets of the world, would now subjugate all opposition, by underselling, until it ruins and destroys that it finally may monopolise and rule the market. It is protection to every trade, calling, enterprise, and industry. All trades are dependent. The farmer lives on the prosperity of the manufacturer, the manufacturer on the wealth of the farmer, the mechanic on the success of each, the labourer on the employment of all.

"The whole people demand protection. Our common prosperity demands it. Labour demands it, for labour is our wealth. Agriculture demands it, for agriculture would be without a market if free trade existed. Why, then, this eternal battle to subjugate our trade to British control? Why this endless theorising against all experience to give control to foreign capital? Why this deathless crusade, which a century of defeats and disasters should have educated into reason, against the broad, full, and comprehensive development of our incomparable resources? If we give up our tariffs we must give up our manufacturing. If we do not protect ourselves, no one will protect us. If labour does not stand by labour, labour will be crushed. Absolute prosperity is when every arm is employed and every mouth is fed. With a tariff for protection, every arm can be employed to enrich into development the incomparable grandeur of our resources. With a tariff for protection, every mouth can be fed with the abundance which is overflowing in the land, if the industry of our land is not forced to give way to the half-paid, half-starved pauperised dependents of Europe."

I have, perhaps, wearied the patience of the reader in quoting these extracts, but which are only a tithe of the entire speech. But this question of Protection is so inseparably linked not only with the fortunes of the country, but with the individual fortunes of those going out to find a home in the New World, that this must be my apology for quoting arguments from the Protectionist side. The entire question resolves itself into a very simple issue; *the consumer pays the tariff*, whatever it is; the manufacturer may be enriched by the system, but it is most certainly at the expense of the community at large, particularly the labouring classes.

There has been, this year (1883), a general revision of the tariffs, which comes into operation on July 1st. Mr. Brewer and his very small party have been instrumental in obtaining an advance in the tariff on pottery. In some commodities there has been a reduction in favour of the manufacturers on this side.

Trenton, as I have said, is a pretty little town, with good streets, and there are shady lanes outside it. Considering all that has been done in Philadelphia, Boston, and New York in the way of schools of design, it is very remarkable that nothing of this kind exists, or at least did at the time of my visit, in Trenton, the chief seat of one of the industries most needing instruction of a technical and artistic character.

CHAPTER XXIII.

MANUFACTURING CENTRES—PATERSON.

AFTER leaving the potteries of Trenton, Paterson, the centre of the silk trade in the States, would, to many, be of interest to visit. Its distance from New York is only about fifteen miles, and it is about the same distance from Trenton. Locomotive making is also carried on in the town, but silk is its leading industry, providing employment for a large portion of its 53,000 inhabitants. It is a clean, well-ordered town, and has as residents and workpeople in it a very large number from Macclesfield, Leek, and Congleton. With a tariff of 60 per cent. for dress, piece and shawl silk, and the same for silk ribbons, the trade has thus been as much nursed as a hothouse plant. Considerable enterprise has been shown for years by those engaged in the trade, and this supported with unlimited capital, and the newest and most improved machinery, has given the silk trade there a status of great influence and importance. This state of things contrasts very forcibly just now with the very unsatisfactory condition of the Macclesfield silk trade, which has for some time past been occupying the serious attention not only of those engaged in it, but of outsiders who have taken no small interest in the various causes which have been alleged for its decline. Many of such out of employment are making their way to Paterson, and becoming quickly absorbed in the increasing number of manufactories there. When crossing to the States in April last, one of my fellow passengers was a Paterson silk dyer, who had been on a visit to Macclesfield, his native place, after an absence of some years. I asked him if he would prefer to have remained in England rather than be returning to Paterson, as he was doing, and his answer was a very decided negative. As a place of residence he said he would prefer Macclesfield, but as for the labour and its relative remuneration, the comparison lay most decidedly, he said, in favour of Paterson. He was, I should remark, evidently a well-skilled artizan, who had, by a thoroughly experienced knowledge, made himself invaluable to his firm, especially in the dyeing of the blended shades, which have been so fashionable.

A correspondent says, in a communication which has just reached my hands, that "there never was a time in the history of America when its textile industries were more tried than now; on the one hand, by competition with the great manufacturing establishments of England (against which our tariff presents but a poor protection for our native labour), and, on the other hand, by the disheartening effects of 'strikes,' which paralyse the efforts of capital and compel the acceptance of foreign products at the expense of our home industries. But, happily, the clouds are lifting, and strikes cease to be prevalent, and the natural consequence will, therefore, be a resumption of energy and an increase of national textile manufacture and a resumption of general prosperity."

There are differences between the methods of manufacture adopted in the States and those in vogue here. Anyone who has visited Macclesfield, Leek, Congleton, and Coventry, would see many evidences of much of the work being done at the house of the operative. In Paterson and Connecticut, where the silk industry is also carried on, all the work is done at the mill.

This work at home is carried on by hand looms, while at the American mills steam power is used in every instance.

One of the greatest difficulties with which silk culture in the

States has had to contend is that of proper reeling. This is not merely mechanical labour, and cannot be performed by any unskilled person. It is an art which requires years of observation, study, and constant practice. Reelers are trained in England, and on the Continent are trained from very early life, and so progress from the ordinary to the more subtle manipulations. This process of reeling, which is one of the primary ones in the silk industry, has been so indifferently done that this has beed a serious drawback in the trade.

The following table of the rates of wages paid per week, compiled 27th April, 1882, by Mr. W. C. Wyckoff, the secretary of the Silk Association of the States, will be interesting, and perhaps of service to those immediately connected with the trade. It was furnished at the request of the Secretary of the U.S. Treasury, and is published in an official document :

Designation of Operative.	Sex.	Average in U.S., 1879, 1880. s. d.	Estimated Average England. s. d.	Estimated Average France. s. d.
Hard silk winder	F.	21 0	12 0	5 8
Hard silk doubler	F.	20 9	—	9 10
Hard silk spinner	M.	20 0	—	8 0
Hard silk twister	M.	24 0	—	13 9
Soft silk winder	F.	25 6	—	8 0
Warper	M.	43 0	—	—
Ditto	F.	30 9	—	9 8
Beamer	M.	48 6	—	—
Weaver on hand looms	M.	56 8	—	21 8
Ditto	F.	33 10	—	12 0
Weaver on power looms	M.	45 10	21 8	—
Ditto	F.	31 0	17 7	—
Finisher	M.	54 0	—	—
Designer	M.	99 0	48 0	—
Lace operative (machine)	M.	59 0	36 6	—
Ditto	F.	20 0	12 0	—
Braid operative	M.	64 0	—	30 0
Braider	F.	21 8	—	30 0
Fringe maker	F.	21 3	—	5 10
Dyer	M.	51 3	28 0	—

He says of the English plan, that "the manufacturer buys filling and warp, which he sends to the dye house, and finally puts it out to weavers who have looms at their own homes. . . . In several of the Paterson mills all the different processes are conducted under a single roof, so that the raw silk becomes finished goods before it leaves the place." In not a few cases the greater part of the machines used in the spinning and weaving of the silk are made on the premises where they are used.

There are few industries in the States which have made a more rapid progress than that of silk, from the culture of the worm to the manufactured article. The conditions for raising silkworms are favourable in most of the States, and many ladies of means and leisure have formed in Philadelphia, San Francisco, and Sacramento, a "Women's Silk Culture Association," and a large quantity of raw silk is thus being placed in the market.

The condition of those engaged in the trade in Paterson is very creditable. The operatives have a comfortable and well-to-do appearance. The cost of living is fully 50 per cent. more than it would be in Macclesfield or Coventry, but notwithstanding this, at the present time they are infinitely better off than hundreds in the English districts referred to.

CHAPTER XXIV.

MANUFACTURING CENTRES—NEWARK.

NEWARK is only ten miles from New York, on the New Jersey side, and only a short distance from Paterson. Its population is 125,000, and its chief trades are cotton manufactures, lead and zinc smelting, saw works, and hat and leather manufacturing. Carriage making and fancy work are also largely carried on. It is the largest city in New Jersey, and is well and substantially built. The city claims to be famed for the beauty of its female population as well as to be an important industrial centre, but of the former fact I was ignorant until after I had left the district. Of the hat manufacture I need now say but little. It is carried on chiefly along the Orange Valley, about a mile or two out of Newark. Many of the works are picturesquely situated, and above and around them are the Orange Mountains. The lower grade qualities of hats occupy the attention of most of the firms engaged in the trade. The wages, take the branches through, are 50 to 100 per cent. higher than in England. This trade in the States is conducted with a great amount of ability and enterprise. Unlimited capital is at the disposal of the leading houses, and there is nothing new or meritorious in the way of labour-saving machinery, either in England or the States, that they have not in work.

Patent and enamelled leather are the chief products of this

industry in Newark, which town, in fact, monopolises this trade, for there is very little carried on elsewhere in America. In this trade tanners are paid 48s. a week, and finishers average 60s. While I am referring to the leather trade it will be convenient here to mention the wages paid in the other branches. These are as follows :

Morocco leather : In New York and Philadelphia tanners are paid 60s. per week ; in Wilmington and Lynn, 40s. per week. Morocco finishers by machinery, New York and Philadelphia, 52s. and 56s. ; and in Lynn, 44s. and 48s. per week. Upper leather and calf skin manufactures : Tanners in Eastern and Western cities, 40s. to 44s. ; and curriers, 52s. and 60s. per week. Wages in the country are less by 8s. to 12s. than in the towns. Sole leather : 5s. per day for tanners, and finishers 6s. to 6s. 6d. per day. In Chicago and other cities tanners earn 36s. to 42s. per week. In each of these cases ten hours is a day's labour.

A well-known Scotch firm of thread manufacturers have large works in Newark, New Jersey, and employ a very large number of females, both young and adults. Mr. W. Clark, one of the principals, says, in a letter sent to the Bureau of Statistics at Washington, on 31st January, 1882 : "With regard to your question as to the effectiveness of labour here and in Paisley, would say that my experience is about equal in both places, and the *employés* in either place, with the same machinery, will produce about the same amount of work, and they work as steadily in one place as in the other. The idea of the superiority of American workmen over British workmen is humbug. It is used when a speaker wants to please an American audience, and generally has the effect he intends. But there is no doubt that both countries have their specialities in which they excel. Cotton spinning and cotton spinning machinery is ahead in Great Britain. and most of our improvements come from there." After careful examination and inquiry, I must say that this view of American labour I can fully endorse. The comparative rates of weekly wages in the thread trade are:

Girls.	Paisley.		Newark.	
	s.	d.	s.	d.
Spoolers	14	6	32	0
Reelers	14	6	32	0
Cop Winders	14	6	32	0
Twisters	9	6	22	0
Slippers	6	9	12	0
Bobbin Cleaners	6	0	10	0

Men.	Paisley.		Newark.	
	s.	d.	s.	d.
Carpenters	29	0	68	0
Machinists	29	0	72	0
Dyers	28	0	60	0
Bleachers	26	0	54	0
Firemen	24	0	50	0

In Newark fifty-nine hours are worked to the week, and in Paisley fifty-five.

CHAPTER XXV.

MANUFACTURING CENTRES—PROVIDENCE AND HARTFORD.

PROVIDENCE is the capital of the State of Rhode Island, and is a perfect beehive of industry. Its population is put down at 104,850. It is very picturesquely situated on Narragansett Bay, with woods and country behind. It was founded originally in 1636 by Roger Williams, a Welshman. The Williams Park contains a very handsome monument to him, executed in granite, and erected in 1877. The industries of the city are numerous, and it has suffered less disaster during the years of financial distress than have many others, an exemption to be attributed to the great variety of trades carried on. In it are numerous cotton factories, such as the Oriental Mills, the Providence Steam Mills, and the Grant Mill; in worsted work, there are the Geneva Worsted Mills, the Providence Worsted Mills, and the Valley Mills for braids, yarns, and hosiery, the Elba and the Weybosset for cashmeres. The manufactures of coatings, boots and shoes, corsets, braids, and twine, with bleaching and dyeing, are also largely carried on. The immense Corliss Engine Works are here, and the factory of Messrs. Willcox and Gibbs would in size and other features surprise many on this side. The making of tools, screws, files, and locomotives, also employs many hands. One of the chief industries of Providence—purposely mentioned last in this extensive list—is the jewellery and silver trade. The production in these goods will, I feel sure, compare favourably with that of any other country. I am, in fact, disposed to doubt at the moment whether Birmingham produces a greater variety of these wares than are made in Providence. When I was in the district in the spring of last year, there was a great demand for silver and jewel chasers, and I was informed that good silver chasers earned as much as £5 per week. This is one of the industries in the States which has made very rapid progress during the last ten years. Both in silver goods and jewellery there is a constant output of novelties noted as much for artistic merit as for the skill with which they are produced. Jewellery is worn universally in the States, and so there is a growing demand which the Providence manufacturers are bent upon keeping pace with. The city itself is a pleasant and healthy one. There are two fresh-water rivers which flow into the Providence salt-water river. Several public buildings of prominence are situated in the principal streets.

The houses are chiefly built of red brick, and very many of these are detached or semi-detached with plenty of trees about them. There is a capital service of both trains and steamboats with New York. The soil generally of Rhode Island is stony, rough, and hard to cultivate; hence throughout the whole island people have turned to other trades, and are absorbed in the many factories and workshops. The population are for the most part clean, industrious, and thrifty.

Johnston, five miles from Providence, is noted for market gardening, but also contains cotton and woollen mills, and at Cranston, six miles away, there is the State prison and asylum for the insane and paupers. Rocky Point, Oatlands Beach, Jamestown Island, which contains a park of 500 acres, are summer and pleasure resorts of the people of Providence. From Sandy Point, a few miles from Providence, there is sometimes observed a phenomenon of flashes of light from the ocean, like the appearance of a ship on fire, supposed to be produced by the same means as the Aurora Borealis.

It will be opportune to give here some tables of wages paid in the various trades referred to. Taking first the cotton trade, the following were the rates paid in 1880 in Massachusetts, New Hampshire, and other places in the New England States:

	Per day of 10 hours. s. d.		Per day of 10 hours. s. d.
Overseer	15 0	Mule spinner	6 5
Second hand	8 0	Warper	3 10
Picker	4 5	Spooler	3 4
Cardstripper	4 0	Dresser	6 6
Frame spinner	3 1	Weaver	3 4

Woollen trade: per day of ten hours in Massachusetts, and eleven hours in New Hampshire and Maine:

	Per day. s. d.		Per day. s. d.
Wool sorting	7 0	Drawing	3 4
Carding	3 0	Weaving	4 1
Spinning	4 10	Gigging	4 0
Spooling	2 3	Finishing	4 0
Dressing	4 9		

In the iron and steel trades, there were in 1880 some 140,978 persons employed. The average daily wages as given in the official returns were 10s. 6d. for skilled labour, and for unskilled labour 5s. The highest average daily wages for skilled labour were paid in Providence and other parts of Rhode Island, Colorado. Taking the Eastern States throughout, the average was—for skilled labour 11s., unskilled 4s. 10d.; Southern States, skilled 10s. 10d., unskilled 4s. 3d.; Western States, skilled 11s., unskilled 5s. 4d.; Pacific States and Territories, skilled 14s., unskilled 7s.

In the rolling mills of Pittsburgh the average has been as follows:

	Per ton. s. d.		Per ton. s. d.
Boiling	20 0	Hoop Rolling and Heating (1in. by No. 18) 16s. to	19 4
Shingling	3 3		
Bar rolling	2 9		
Heating	2 9	Sheet Rolling and Heating (No. 24)	28 8
Guide rolling rounds and squares ½in.	9 8		

The wages in tanneries in Pennsylvania and New York are:

	Per day of 10 hours. s. d.		Per day of 10 hours. s. d.
Beam hand	5 3	Bark Grinder	4 6
Yard hand	5 0	Labourer	4 6
Roller	5 0		

Sole leather tanners in Philadelphia, Baltimore, &c., earn 36s. to 42s. per week.

Sole leather tanners in the county towns get 5s. per day, and sole leather curriers 6s. to 6s. 6d. per day, working 10 hours to the day.

Hartford (Connecticut) is another of the very many important manufacturing centres of the States, being noted for its iron and brass ware, steam-engines and boilers, sewing machines, fire-arms, mechanics' tools, screws, silver-plated ware, stoneware, silk, woollens, envelopes, cigars, fertilisers, and a vast number of other productions, in common parlance, too numerous to mention. There are also several large factories for bedsteads and wire mattresses. It is situated 109 miles from New York, and has a population of 42,553. Some twelve to fifteen square miles are comprised by the town. Park River intersects it, and this is spanned by eleven or twelve bridges. There is also a bridge across the River Connecticut, 1000ft. long, which connects the city proper with East Hartford. The city is well built, and has a more finished appearance than many other American towns. I may say that this peculiarity applies to most of the towns in the New England States. The New State House, built of marble, in the Gothic style, is a very fine building, 300ft. long by 200ft. wide, and 250ft. high to the top of the dome. The City Hall, Post Office, the Union Railway Depôt, Trinity College, and the Wadsworth Athenæum, would all be objects of interest to the visitor.

The Colt's Firearms Manufactory and the Willow Works form quite an important district in the S.E. portion of the city. There is no great difficulty in English visitors seeing over some parts of these works, and they could scarcely fail to be interesting to all. Some very pretty drives surround Hartford. Hartford, I may mention, is one of the chief centres of fire and life insurance business. The offices of some of these companies are very handsome structures.

The hotel charges are the same as in other cities, viz., 12s. to 16s. per day.

CHAPTER XXVI.

GENERAL IMPRESSIONS.

It will, of course, be at once acknowledged that it is only by a lengthened stay in any country that a trustworthy and comprehensive idea of it can be obtained. Even in brief visits, however, some impressions must be formed by every one, and succeeding visits strengthen or remove these impressions. The former was my own case. Of the vastness of the country across the Atlantic we on this side are far from having anything like a definite idea. Mere size is scarcely a merit in itself, and with our cousins it has the effect of requiring everything worth considering to have this characteristic. Churches and shows, railways and manufactories, rivers and waterfalls, failures and wealth, all must be on a gigantic scale to be equal to the American notion of things in general, and some things in particular. Yield them this fact of immensity—a very prolific word in the American vocabulary—and they will overlook criticism on other features. Breathing and elbow room is the first feeling that most people who visit the country become conscious of. Excepting in the largest cities, the houses and manufactories are scattered over a large area, and this could scarcely be otherwise, considering the large space at disposal. The mileage of some of the railways and the area of some of the States will be interesting, and, according to a table

General Impressions.

compiled on Jan. 1st, 1882, the railway mileage of the various States and Territories was as follows :

	Miles.		Miles.
Illinois	8,326	Mississippi	1,232
Pennsylvania	6,690	Maryland and D.C.	1,048
Ohio	6,664	Arkansas	1,042
New York	6,279	New Hampshire	1,026
Iowa	6,113	Maine	1,022
Texas	5,344	Louisiana	999
Indiana	4,765	New Mexico Territory	975
Michigan	4,284	Connecticut	959
Missouri	4,211	Vermont	916
Kansas	3,718	Utah Territory	908
Wisconsin	3,442	Nevada	890
Minnesota	3,391	Florida	793
Georgia	2,581	West Virginia	712
Nebraska	2,310	Oregon	689
Colorado	2,275	Arizona Territory	557
California	2,261	Wyoming Territory	533
Virginia	2,194	Washington Territory	480
Tennessee	1,974	Delaware	278
Massachusetts	1,935	Indian Territory	275
Alabama	1,804	Idaho Territory	265
New Jersey	1,753	Montana Territory	232
Kentucky	1,715	Rhode Island	211
Dakota Territory	1,639		
North Carolina	1,619	Total miles	104,813
South Carolina	1,484		

The area of the leading States and Territories is given below :

	Square Miles.		Square Miles.
New York	49,170	Maryland	12,210
Pennsylvania	45,215	New Hampshire	9,305
North Carolina	52,250	Kentucky	40,400
South Carolina	30,570	Maine	33,040
Georgia	59,475	Missouri	69,415
Arkansas	53,850	Texas	265,780
California	158,360	Nevada	110,700
Nebraska	76,855	Minnesota	83,365
New Mexico	122,580	Dakota	149,100
Alaska	577,390	Arizona	113,020

The trite saying of "facts being stubborn things" is especially true with regard to such statistics as those now quoted. We in England read them with amazement, and cannot wonder that our cousins should "talk large" now and then. I believe that for America there is a grand future. She has much to contend with in the teeming millions pouring into her country. Heterogeneous as is the mass, it may safely be said that the majority are turned into peaceable, industrious, and law-abiding citizens.

The friction of life between class and class is less than with us. There is no class looked down upon. The artisan population holds a powerful position in the country, and there is no doubt whatever but that there is among them more sobriety, and a far more general endeavour to meet the wishes of employers than with us. There has been, without doubt, on the other side of the Atlantic, a larger uplifting of the masses than with us. Educational and religious matters are conducted with a vigour that in some respects we would do well to copy in this country. Public and private philanthropy is carried on to an extent that were some facts quoted, which might be, they would be surprising to many. Almost every want of mankind in this country has been cared for.

If in commercial life there is not an infrequent exhibition of "smartness," there are on the other hand thousands of business firms conducted with as much uprightness and conscientiousness as can be found in any part of Great Britain, and in addition to these qualities there is withal far more enterprise and spirit thrown into their business than may be found in any other part of the world. This is not evident merely in puffing advertisements and self-laudation, but in the practical and thorough way that they have in going about things.

The Americans, especially in the New England and immediately surrounding States, are a genial and hospitable people. They are ever ready to extend a warm welcome to English people, and in the affairs of our country they take the liveliest interest. Our prominent statesmen are through their newspapers almost as familiar to them as to us. The American press always gives English news liberally, and there is, happily for both countries, an improved tone observable in their columns when dealing with English matters.

Intemperance is far less common among all classes than with us. Lager beer, it is true, is consumed in large quantities, but this is a light, unintoxicating drink. Cases of drunkenness along the streets are not by any means common. This alone shows a great advance on the old country. There is no room in factories for drunken workmen, and many an English artisan who takes this bad habit with him has to move about from situation to situation, for he can find few masters who will put up with such conduct longer than it will take to find another man to fill his place.

I am strongly disposed to think that labour troubles in America are her inheritance for the next few years. We have in this country been watching the strikes in the iron and other trades. Labour organisations for various industries are less general than with us, but the " Knights of Labour " movement has given trouble during the last year or two, and will give more trouble as it gathers strength. The original object of this and many other trade organisations was a form of benefit society, but latterly they have added to their action all the power and objects known to trades' unions here. In some trades in the States masters are compelling their operatives to sign agreements, that during the time they are in their employ they will not become members of the Knights of Labour league or any other such organisation. The gist of this document is as follows:

"I, A B, agree to work for C D at my trade, for the regularly established prices, doing my work in a good workmanlike manner; withdrawing from the Knights of Labour and ignoring all outside parties, committees, and trade or labour associations; and I also agree not to connect myself with the Knights of Labour or any similar organisation, or to join in any meeting or procession of such organisations while in the employ of the said C D. In consideration of which the said C D agrees to pay the said A B for his services every two weeks as customary—necessary stoppages excepted. The above agreement can only be terminated by either party giving to the other two weeks' notice, unless for bad workmanship, violation of this contract or the rules of the factory, or for interference with other workmen."

The working classes have hitherto been so scattered that they have scarcely had the opportunity to organise themselves into unions, but centralisation is going on at such a rapid rate that it is giving them the opportunity of doing so, and they are setting about it with a determination which bodes evil in the future.

The Americans are essentially a practical people. If you enter a store to make a purchase, there is invariably an undemonstrative demeanour on the part of the salesman (or clerk, as he is termed), which contrasts somewhat with the attention generally bestowed in the shops of the metropolis. This must not be construed into a feeling of indifference or disrespect on the part of the salesman, but is part of their system, which assumes without its being claimed, that there is no social inferiority between the wealthy merchant and landowner, and the labourer or clerk. There is also the further reason that the salesman credits the customer with the desire to have his business well and promptly done, and so pays no compliments, but attends at once to what he is asked for. Many business men, again, on this side would delight at the quick way in which both large and small buyers make up their minds as to what they require. There is on this side a great amount of hesitancy and indecision, often very trying, and we might with advantage follow more generally the quick dispatch with which the Americans execute their business.

There are natural resources of America scarcely yet touched.

The amount of mineral wealth is alone incalculable, and will provide millions of money in years to come, but the opening up and developing of these interests is a question of years. The progress of America, commercially, dates back only some ten to twenty years, and what the next ten years will reveal in further progress remains to be seen. There need, however, be no jealousy between the United States and England, for each, I do not fear, will be able to hold her own; and at present, with her tariffs on raw materials, we have no reason to fear the competition of American manufacturers in foreign markets which we have hitherto largely controlled. One advantage the Americans have in their favour, and that is, that in whatever part of the world there is business to be done they will not be long in placing someone there to do it. The Americans may be said to live to travel, and the English to travel to live.

American consuls are officially the Government representatives, in their various districts, but in reality the resident agents of American manufacturers, and being in most cases men of business, they take up commercial interests as a matter of course; whilst our own consuls are retired colonels and captains, or the sons of the aristocracy, not particularly interested in business, and as for their reports, as a rule supposed to be of value, it is usually twelve months or so before they are published in blue-book form, and then they are of very little service to the British trading class. It is greatly astonishing that this should be the case in regard to a country which can reasonably claim to be the most commercial in the world.

I have a growing conviction that a marked improvement is taking place in the tone of society both in the States and in England. The feeling of friendship has been cemented during the last year or two, and never were these two vast English-speaking countries more in accord one with another than at the present time. That this feeling may not only continue but deepen should be the wish of all right-minded people. There is no doubt that England and America combined are exercising more moral power than all the other countries of the world put together, and they are the great civilising forces of the future. George Washington, over a hundred years ago, said that the forming of that country into an independent State was an experiment, and so far the experiment has proved a most successful one. That there are some dangers ahead will be readily admitted by all Americans, and by all who have visited the country, but of what country can this not be said?

CHAPTER XXVII.

WHO SHOULD EMIGRATE.

PUBLIC attention has been so generally turned towards America during the years of commercial depression in this country, now happily passed, or nearly so, that such a question as the above has been asked over and over again, and received a variety of answers. America is not by any means an Eldorado for all. There could be found in New York as much poverty as there is in London, and the overcrowding of dwelling-houses in the districts inhabited by the working classes would provide in many cases quite as appalling facts as could be found in St. Giles's or Whitechapel. There are at the present time in the leading cities of the States quite as many unemployed as may be found in many English towns. There has been some exaggeration in the prospects held out to those who contemplate finding a new home, and there are some industries which are greatly overdone in America. It is just as possible to do well in England as America; and success there is dependent on just the same qualities as are necessary here. Of unskilled labour there is enough and to spare in America. The old saying must again be used, that a man with a trade in his hands stands a hundred per cent. better chance there than one who has not. American industries are progressing at a rapid rate, and there is room in them for men of skill and industry, with good remuneration for their work, and a social position higher than would be their corresponding status here. Whatever a man's trade is in the States is no barrier to his social progress. Labour is honoured highly, as all the world over it ought to be, if honestly followed.

My own view is that, comparing the two countries, there is a better and quicker return for the same amount of capital or labour in the States than is possible in the majority of cases here.

The feeling that there is scope in the States obtains possession of the mind of the man who goes out determined to make his way. Willingness to work and to take the work which presents itself ought to be dominant. Several cases come to my mind that I know personally. A friend of mine had an excellent training as a mechanical engineer, crossed the Atlantic, and is doing favourably as a store keeper and small farmer, killing his pigs himself and taking all such work as part of the day's labour. Another was unsuccessful in business on his own account, in one of the midland towns of England, and is now a manager of works in the trade in which he was engaged here, at an excellent salary, and bids fair to be a partner by-and-bye, without any large investment, his knowledge and skill in the business being accepted as the equivalent of capital. For those who have good situations in this country, to give them up for the sake of change, with the idea of doing better out there, is not by any means advisable. On the other hand, for unmarried young men, with plenty of energy, and who like work for its own sake, there is plenty of room; and such, with tact, push and principle, the great motto of Abraham Lincoln, would scarcely fail to get on.

Let me here give one practical suggestion to those who contemplate going out and who have a trade in their hands. Advertise for what employment you are seeking in the journal representing your particular trade. Class papers are prolific in America, and are largely read, and used for the purpose of bringing employer and employé together.

America is full of schoolmasters, tutors, professors of music, languages, and other arts. For clever and original designers there is a demand. In the engineering and hardware trade there is a good scope. The chemical industries are rapidly developing, and those who have a good and trustworthy knowledge of the making of chemicals for manufacturing purposes would find room for their labours. I have already referred to the jewellery and silver trade. The shirt, collar, and clothing trades are overstocked, excepting, perhaps, as regards hats. Saddlery and harness makers find remunerative employment. Printers are in demand, but, before such could find good employment, they would require to get well accustomed to the American ideas of display. In the Birmingham and Sheffield trades there are openings for labour.

With whatever capital a person emigrates, and none should go without some, he should prefer to err in being over cautious rather than prematurely confident. There are all manner of methods for ridding a new comer of his stock of wealth if he be not wide awake. A short time spent in reconnoitring after arrival would be advisable to most, but in few cases is it well to attempt settling down in New York. Other cities present far better opportunities than that one, which unfortunately receives a good deal of scum from every part of the world.

I know nothing of the value of land and the practical prospects of farming, but I do know that farming there is very different from what it is here. It may be rough and primitive there when compared with scientific farming here, but it is, at all events, more likely of success. Untold millions of acres yet remain to be cultivated, and here I will quote a few figures. Of the 220,000,000 acres of land in Ohio, Indiana, Illinois, Michigan, and Wisconsin, about 90,000,000 are under cultivation, and 70,000,000 consists of forests and sandy plains, the other 60,000,000 being still available for colonisation. There are in the States of Kansas, Nebraska, and Minnesota 160,000,000 acres, 12,000,000 of which are under cultivation, while 78,000,000 might be cultivated at a large profit and a very small preliminary outlay. Texas has 200,000,000 acres, but the greater part has hitherto been used chiefly for grazing, yet there are at least 60,000,000 acres which might with advantage be planted with corn and cotton. In the territories of Montana, Wyoming, and Dakota there are about 120,000,000 acres of very good land, nearly the whole of which is at present uncultivated and can be obtained on very easy terms.

In the purchasing of land every care and caution will require to be exercised. The literature of the various land companies must not always be accepted without question. They naturally speak graphically and enthusiastically about what they are desirous of selling.

In the towns living is very much dearer than in England. Money has not the same purchasing value there as here. Rents are notoriously high, and it may safely be said that an average rent in New York would swallow up of itself an average salary on this side.

The immense increase in the emigration returns for the last few years, from what can be gathered, has not perceptibly overstocked the market. Some writers in Germany have been making a great deal recently of the fact of some German emigrants returning to their native districts with disappointed hopes, but it is patent that official Germany does not relish this drain of the bone and sinew of the country, glad to find a home in the Far West where conscription cannot follow them.

The population of the United States at the last census was 50,155,783, and there is yet room for some five or six times the number, so far as the size of the country is concerned. For her vast absorbing power Europe owes a debt of gratitude to her, and she is fulfilling her duty to Europe very faithfully, and to British people especially she holds out a very welcome hand.

CHAPTER XXVIII.

TARIFF CHARGES AND TABLE OF DISTANCES, &c.

The following list of the tariff charges on some leading commodities will be useful, not only to such as may contemplate going out to the States, but to those on this side. It should be borne in mind that the charges must be paid by the purchaser, so that the amount must be added to what the article would cost in this country. The American-made article is only in some few instances sold cheaper than the imported article.

As mentioned in a former chapter, the tariff has been considerably modified; on some manufactures there has been a reduction, and on others an increase. The new rates were appointed to come into operation on July 1st, 1883, and they are now given as revised. To give the United States tariff in its entirety would, of itself, fill a book, and I mention only those articles which intending emigrants and tourists are likely to take with them.

The Taxed List.

Animals: Living	20 per cent.
Books	25 ,,
Boots and shoes	35 ,,
Bronze, manufactures of	35 ,,
Carpets: Axminster and all woven whole for room	45 cents per sq. yard, and 30 per cent.
,, Brussels tapestry	30 cents per sq. yard, and 30 per cent.

A Tour in the States and Canada.

Carpets: Velvet, patent or tapestry	25 cents per sq. yard, and 30 per cent.
Carriages	35 per cent.
Clocks	30 ,,
China: Porcelain and Parian ware, plain	55 ,,
,, gilded, or decorated	50 ,,
Clothing, wholly or in part of wool	50 cents per lb., and 40 per cent.
,, silk component	60 per cent.
,, all other descriptions	35 ,,
Cutlery, table, &c.	35 ,,
,, Pen and pocket knives	50 ,,
Diamonds and other precious stones, set	25 ,,
,, unset	10 ,,
Engravings	25 ,,
Furniture, Furs, manufacture	35 ,,
Gilt and plated ware	35 ,,
Guns	35 ,,
Glass ware, plain, mould or pressed	35 ,,
,, cut, engraved, gilt, painted	40 ,,
Gold and silver ware	40 ,,
Gloves, kid	50 ,,
Hats, straw	40 ,,
,, trimmed with silk and artificial flowers, exceeding the value of the hat	60 ,,
,, with feathers and artificial flowers	50 ,,
Hosiery, cotton	35 ,,
,, silk	60 ,,
,, wool	35 ,,
Jewellery, gold, silver or imitation	25 ,,
,, jet	25 ,,
Laces, silk and cotton	60 ,,
,, thread	30 ,,
Leather, manufactures of	35 ,,
Linen, table, towelling, &c.	35 to 40 per cent.
Machinery, brass or iron	35 per cent.
,, copper or steel	45 ,,
Medicinal preparations	40 ,,
Musical instruments	30 ,,
Music, printed	20 ,,
Paintings	10 ,,
Frames	25 ,,
Photographs	25 ,,
Saddles and harness	35 ,,
Shawls, wool	50 cents per b. and 40 per cent.
Silk, dress piece, shawls	60 per cent.
Soap, fancy, perfumed, toilet	10 cents per lb. and 35 per cent.
Stereoscopic views on paper	25 per cent.

Stereoscopic views on glass	40 per cent.
Spirits, brandy, gin, and whiskey	2dols. per proof gallon.
Umbrella, silk or alpaca	50 per cent.
Velvet, silk	60 ,,
,, cotton	35 ,,
Watches	25 ,,
Wines	from 40 cents per gallon to 24s. per doz.

It will be seen from the foregoing list that it is not the luxuries of life which are the most heavily taxed. Diamonds are 10 per cent., but the most important necessaries of life, such as clothing, 35 per cent., and blankets 100 per cent.

THE FREE LIST.

The following articles are exempt from duty :

Books, engravings, bound or unbound, etchings, maps, and charts, which shall have been printed and manufactured more than twenty years at the date of importation.

Professional books of those intending to remain in the country.

Cabinets of coins, medals, and all other collections of antiquities.

Newspapers and periodicals, philosophical and scientific apparatus, instruments, and preparations, statuary casts in marble, bronze, alabaster, or plaster of Paris, paintings, drawings, and etchings for scientific and literary purposes, and not intended for sale.

CHARGES FOR WASHING LINEN, &C.

The cost of washing and getting up linen, either in hotels or boarding houses, is as follows:

Shirts	6½d. each	Collars	1½d. each
,, with collars ...	7½d. ,,	Cuffs	3d. per pair
Shirt fronts with collars		Socks	3d. ,,
attached	6½d. ,,	Neck ties ...	1½d. ,,
Under shirts	6½d. ,,	Dust Coats ...	1s. to 1s. 6d. each
Night shirts	6½d. ,,	Pants	1s. each
Drawers	6½d. ,,	Vests	1s. to 1s. 6d. each
Handkerchiefs	3d. ,,		

DISTANCES FROM NEW YORK OF VARIOUS TOWNS AND CITIES, POPULATION, ETC.

Town	State	Popula- tion—1880 Census.	Distance from New York.	Fare.		Manufactures.
			Miles.	s.	d.	
Addison	N.Y.	4,000	302	31	0	
Adrian	Mich.	8,869	817	73	0	Iron Foundries, Car Building, Woollen and Flour Mills.
Albany	N.Y.	90,903	143	12	5	Railway Depôts, Agricultural Implements.
Alexandria	Va.	14,000	233	26	0	
Alleghany City	Pa.	65,010	445	42	0	
Allentown	Pa.	18,200	92	11	0	Iron Mills, Foundries.
Altoona	Pa.	20,000	327	37	10	Locomotive and Machine Shops, Foundries.
Amsterdam	N.Y.	11,800	176	15	0	
Arthison	Kan.	15,000	1390	149	0	Woollen Factories, Flour Mills.
Atlanta	Ga.	46,500	878	130	0	Woollen Mills, Planing and Rolling Mills.
Auburn	N.Y.	22,000	317	26	0	Wheel Works.
Augusta	Ga.	27,000	808	126	0	Iron Foundries.
Austin	Tex.	20,000	1907	236	0	
Baltimore	Md.	330,000	188	25	0	Shipping and Lumber Port, Saw Works.
Bangor	Me.	19,000	464	50	0	
Bath	Me.	10,000	406	39	0	
Belleville	Ont.	9,500	502	50	6	Iron and Steel Works, Zinc Smelting.
Bethlehem	Pa.	12,000	93	10	0	
Binghampton	N.Y.	18,200	285	29	6	Cotton, Woollen, Organ Building, &c.
Boston	Mass.	352,000	229	20	0	Ironworks, Sewing Machines, Carriage Building.
Bridgeport	Conn.	23,000	56	5	0	
Brookline	Mass.	10,000	225	24	0	
Buffalo	N.Y.	150,000	423	37	0	Ship Building, Steel and Iron Works, Timber Yards.
Burlington	Iowa	30,000	1150	117	0	
Cambridge	Mass.	50,000	220	20	0	Brick Making, Woodware.
Camden	N.J.	37,000	89	10	0	Iron Foundries, Bottleworks, Smelting.
Chelsea	Mass.	21,050	245	25	0	Copper Mining, Steel Works, Axe Works.
Chester	Pa.	23,000	112	12	0	Various.
Chicago	Ill.	499,000	899	88	0	Iron Works, Hardware, Boots and Shoes, Soap and Candle Making, Pottery.
Cincinnati	O.	255,804	744	80	0	Petroleum Refining, Hammer Works, Iron Works.
Cleveland	O.	158,000	581	57	0	Hats.
Columbus	Ga.	16,000	1016	111	0	Iron Works, Woollen and Flour Mills, Car and Wagon Building.
Crestline	O.	25,000	633	66	0	Iron Works, Agricultural Machinery, Varnish Making.
Danbury	Conn.	10,000	66	6	6	
Denver	Col.	34,000	1980	256	0	
Detroit	Mich.	109,000	679	73	0	Sewing Machines, Tool Shops.
Dubuque	Iowa.	25,500	1101	111	0	Iron Works.
Elizabeth	N.J.	28,229	12	1	3	
Elmira	N.Y.	21,500	305	29	0	

Tariff Charges and Table of Distances, &c.

City	State				Industries
Erie	Pa.	28,000	510	47	Foundries, Agricultural Implements.
Evansville	Ind.	38,500	999	112	
Fall River	Mass.	46,000	200	22	Cotton and Woollen Mills, Bleaching.
Frankford	Pa.	20,000	83	10	
Galveston	Texas	36,000	1691	285	
Grand Rapids		40,000	937	79	
Hamilton	Ont.	34,000	487	43	
Hartford	Vt.	41,000	148	19	
Holyoke	Mass.	20,000	144	16	Paper Making, Cotton and Woollen Factories.
Houston	Harris Co.	25,000	1741	232	
Indianapolis	Ind.	77,000	812	81	Brass and Iron Foundries.
Ithaca	N. Y.	12,000	280	30	(Cornell University.)
Jersey City	N. J.	116,000	1	1	Zinc Smelting, Woollen and Print Works.
Kansas City	Mo.	65,000	1340	149	Coal, Lumber, Agricultural Implements, Machine Shops.
Lancaster	Pa.	30,000	159	18	Cotton, Woollen, and Worsted Mills.
Lawrence	Mass.	35,000	200	29	
Lewiston	Me.	18,000	379	41	
London	Ont.	26,000	563	52	
Lynchburg	Va.	18,000	405	77	Ship Building, Cotton, Oil.
Memphis	Tenn.	60,000	1159	146	
Meriden	Conn.	19,000	91	9	Lumber, Iron Works, Woodware.
Milwaukee	Wis.	130,000	1046	100	Flour and Saw Mills.
Minneapolis	Minn.	45,000	1381	145	
Montreal	Canada	110,000	400	48	
Morrisania	N. Y.	20,000	7	1	Flour, Saw, and Planing Mills, Paper Mills.
Nashville	Tenn.	35,000	1052	126	Cotton, Lead, Saw Works.
Newark	N. J.	125,000	10	0	
New Brunswick	N. J.	20,000	32	10	Hats.
Norristown	Pa.	15,000	105	2	
Norwalk	Conn.	13,500	43	11	
Norwich	Conn.	21,141	137	4	Woollen Mills, Paper and Flour Mills.
Oshkosh	Wis.	20,000	1126	113	Thread.
Pawtucket	R. I.	20,000	190	20	Salmon Tinning, Grain Shipping, Lumber Trade.
Portland	Org.	20,500	4500	—	Shipping Port for Grain, Machine Works, and Foundries.
Portland	Me.	32,500	337	36	Coal, Iron Works, Hardware.
Reading	Pa.	43,000	134	12	Iron Works, Tobacco, Foundries.
Richmond	Va.	80,000	314	46	Cotton, Saw Works, Machine Shops.
Rochester	N. Y.	90,000	385	30	Beef Packing, Iron Foundries, Woodware, Tobacco, Zinc Smelting, Whitelead Making, &c.
Saint Joseph	Mo.	35,000	1374	149	Lumber and Flour Mills, Foundries.
St. Louis	Mo.	350,522	1098	116	Woollen Mills, Copper Rolling, Machine Shops, &c.
St. Paul	Minn.	42,000	1371	144	
San Francisco	Col.	300,000	3404	552	Iron Mills, Paper Collar Manufactories.
Saratoga	N. Y.	10,000	181	16	
Springfield	Mass.	31,300	135	13	
Stonington	Conn.	65,000	136	17	Iron, Flour Mills, Breweries, Paper, Furniture, &c.
Toronto	Ont.	70,000	527	47	Shirts, Collars, &c.
Troy	N. Y.	55,000	149	12	Shipping Port, Turpentine Works, Cotton, Saw and Planing Mills.
Wilmington	Del.	42,000	118	12	

Care should, at all times, be exercised in addressing letters to America, that the name of the State is given, as there are many towns and cities of the same name in different States.

I have now only to thank my readers who have followed me thus far, and trust that I may have been of some service, not only to those who have an immediate prospect of going out, but to others who are looking forward to spending a holiday at some future time in a visit to the great, beautiful, and progressive country on the other side of the Atlantic. I would again repeat, as a last word, that a trip to America and back is as much within the reach of thousands of business men as is a scamper over the Continent, and for real interest and freshness, the former is preferable to the latter.

FINIS.

INDEX.

A

	PAGE
Albany	41
Alexandria	111
Atlantic, across the	5

B

	PAGE
Baltimore	102
Buildings, principal	104
Hotels	104
Places of interest in	103
Boston	43
Buildings, principal	45, 47
Cab fares	45
Hotels	44
Places of interest in	45
Streets, principal	46
Suburbs of	49
Bradford	94
Brooklyn	36
Buffalo	74
Buildings, principal	75
Hotels	75
Burning Spring	73

C

	PAGE
Cab fares, Boston	45
Fares, New York	30
Cambridge	49
Catskill	41
Charges, tariff	161
Chandière Falls	62, 64
Chicago	79
Buildings, principal	83
Hotels	82
Industries of	81
Cincinnati	85
Buildings, principal	86
Hotels	87
Places of interest in	87
Cleveland	75
Buildings, principal	76
Hotels	76
Concord	50
Coney Island	37

D

	PAGE
De Cheyne Rapids	65

Index.

	PAGE
Detroit	76
Buildings, principal	77
Hotels	78
Distances from New York of various towns, table of	164

E

Emigrate, who should	157
Exeter	52

F

Falls of Niagara	69
Far Rockaway	37
Fare on Cunard Company's steamers	7

G

Garfield	98
General impressions	150—156
Georgetown	111
Glen Falls	41

H

Harrod's Creek	88
Hartford	148
Buildings, principal	148
Industries of	148
Horseshoe Falls	71
Hotels, American	18
And Hotel Life	18
Baltimore	104

	PAGE
Hotels, Boston	44
Buffalo	75
Chicago	82
Cincinnati	87
Cleveland	76
Cost of living at American	19
Detroit	79
Fare in American	20
Life in American	23
Montreal	52
New York	25
Niagara	69
Philadelphia	122
Pittsburgh	92
Quebec	62
Richmond	102
St. Louis	91
Toronto	67
Washington	111
Hudson, up the	39

I

Impressions, general	150—156
Introduction	1
Isle of Orleans	62

J

Jeffersonville	88
Johnston	146

L

Lachine Rapids	58
Landing, arrangements on	15

Index.

	PAGE
Lexington	88
Long Branch	38
Louisville...	87
Buildings, principal ...	88
Luggage, necessary	13
Lynn	50

M

Manhattan Beach	38
Manufacturing centres	128—149
Milwaukee ...	85
Money, American ...	14
Montmorenci, Falls of	62
Montreal	51
Buildings, principal	55
Hotels	52
Mount Vernon	111

N

New Albany	88
Haven	44
York, buildings, principal	33
York cab fares ...	30
York hotels	22
York, places of interest in	33—36
York, sights	30
York, streets, principal	32
York, suburbs of	36
York tram fares	31
Newark	142
Industries of ...	142
Niagara Falls ...	69
Hotels	69

O

	PAGE
Oil City	97
Regions, the ...	94
Ottawa	63
Buildings, principal ...	63

P

Passage, cost of	7
Paterson	138
Industries of	138
Peekskill	40
Pennsylvania	123
Philadelphia	112
Buildings, principal	114—122
Hotels	122
Places of interest in	115—122
Pittsburgh	91
Hotels ...	92
Portland	52
Poughkeepsie	41
Providence	145
Industries of	145

Q

Quebec	61
Buildings, principal ...	62
Hotels	62

R

Railroad scenery of Pennsylvania	123
Railways, American	25
American, baggage system on	27
Rapids, shooting the ...	57

	PAGE
Richmond	101
Buildings, principal	102
Hotels	102
Places of interest in	102
Rideau Falls	65
Rockaway Beach	37

S

	PAGE
St. Lawrence, River	58
St. Louis	89
Buildings, principal	90
Hotels	91
Industries of	91
Places of interest in	90
Saratoga Springs	41
Sea-sickness, preventatives of	10
Shooting the Rapids	57
Silver Creek	88
Staten Island	38
Steamer, amusements on board	10
Choice of	5

T

	PAGE
Table of distances from New York	164
Tariff charges	161
Tarrytown	40
Titusville	98
Toronto	66
Buildings, principal	67
Hotels	67
Tram fares at New York	31
Trenton	128
Industries of	128

W

	PAGE
Washington	105
Buildings, principal	106
Hotels	111
Places of interest in	106
Westchester	40
West Point	40
Who should emigrate	157

www.ingramcontent.com/pod-product-compliance
Lightning Source LLC
Chambersburg PA
CBHW032154160426
43197CB00008B/905